CW00519927

BLED

SLOVENIA

2018
Standard Edition

A Firsthand Guide

Davy Sims

ISBN: 9781977025357

www.firsthandguides.co.uk

In association with

Lake Bled News

www. LakeBledNews.com

@LakeBledNews

手

Firsthand Guides

This is the May 2018 edition of Firsthand Guide's Bled, Slovenia and supersedes and replaces the March edition which has now been withdrawn. At the time of publication, the information is correct. However, additional updates will be added as the year progresses when deemed necessary.

With thanks to Tatjana Radovič for all her kindness, encouragement and expertise on great places to lunch in Ljubljana.

Contents

INTRODUCTION

Bled attracts visitors of all ages, interests and tastes. While many arrive in organised groups, increasingly large numbers come independently for a day, a weekend, a week and sometimes even longer. In 2017 there were 1 million overnight stays in this small town.

Some people see Bled as a short stopover, just a few hours to visit to the castle, take a short voyage on a pletna to explore the Bled Island, perhaps do a circuit of the lake in a horse drawn carriage. Some only get a snapshot by arriving in coaches to spend a very short time.

This guide is aimed at all and any of those people. Whether you spend an afternoon or a week in Bled, this book aims to help you find the best, the hidden and the most exciting aspects of the town whether that be food, drinks, activities, entertainment or sights.

I mainly speak directly to the reader and assume you are – even in an organised group – "independent"; that is, you decide what you want to do and where you want to go, are happy to explore something new and don't mind a few words of advice from people who have been before you and are now coming back.

To that end, we travel together and independently.

"Every morning, I walk around the lake to my office. Bled is my hometown, but I admire its beauties everyday even more."

Lea Ferjan – Bled Culture Institute

INTRODUCTION
to 2018 Edition

2018 A year of Culture

2018 is the European Year of Cultural Heritage and Slovenia is anticipating a year of cultural tourism. Bled is an important part of the county's heritage – the lake, the castle, the island, the pletna and even Bled cream cake. Many of the events held each year are part of the country's and the region's cultural heritage. As are the classical music of Festival Bled to the celebration of the accordion held at the beginning of May each year to the rowing and skiing events to the Taste Bled menus each summer and so many other occasions, big and small.

There are many other cultural attributes that can be associated with Bled including the national poet Prešeren who described the region in the epic poem The Baptism at The Savica where he writes about the waves surrounding the island and the pilgrims on their journey. He talks about the snow-capped mountains in the background, the castle, the fields in summer and ends by saying

> "The land of Carniola does not have a more beautiful place,
> when surrounded by this, the image of paradise.

The Prešeren House is in the village of Vrba in the Municipality of Žirovnica about an hour's walk from Bled, or 10 minutes by car and bus. France Prešeren was born here in 1800. You can visit most days; it is closed on Mondays. His home and work place in Kranj, Prešernova hiša, is in the old town near the tourist information centre at Prešernova ulica 7, 4000 Kranj. Phone: 386 51 615 388

For a translation of the poem and more about Prešeren go to the website *www.preseren.net*

Bees and beekeeping

From 2018 onwards, the United Nations will recognise 20 May each year as World Bee Day. It has taken three years' work to convince the UN of the importance of beekeeping (or apiculture). The campaign was led by Slovenia where one in every 200 people is a beekeeper. The official word came just before Christmas 2017 when an official government announcement said, "Slovenia sees this confirmation of its efforts above all as an obligation to do even more to protect bees and to be even more active in ensuring biodiversity."

The importance of bee keeping and the influence of bees to all our environments is only just being understood. This part of Slovenia is the home of the Carniolan honeybee the second most common bee species in the world. The Museum of Apiculture is in Radovljica, has a very impressive collection of historic painted beehive panels depicting images from the life at the foot of the Alps. Some are well over 100 years old. There are beehives in the shape of a giant man and a doll's house. Radovljica with its tiny but beautiful old town is 10 minutes from Bled by bus.

Throughout this book there are many examples of Slovenian culture; music, wine, food and festivals. Yet Slovenia's most important cultural asset is the people. Almost always friendly – there are a few exceptions anywhere in the world – almost always interested in you, where you came from, that you think of Slovenia, excited (well, usually amused) if you try to speak Slovenian.

Slovenians especially people in Carniola are cultured, they enjoy the outdoors, they are very family focused. If you engage with them, they usually will engage with you.

When that happens you really enjoy the country.

Davy Sims

21 May 2018

PART 1 –
THE HARD FACTS

What's new for 2018?

Water, water everywhere – and plenty for all to drink. New water fountains are being introduced – you can find one at the road below the Town Hall, for example. As well as making drinking water available for all, it should reduce the use of plastic bottles.

A scheme "Ask Me I'm a Local" is to be introduced.

The 1st Bled Wine Festival will be held in August. There are details in the Wine section of this book

Traffic has been something of a problem at the height of the season, so there are to be new measures to help relieve the problem. The municipality will build a new parking lot this summer. It will be temporarily and mainly for coaches but will be expanded to take cars in autumn 2018 and spring 2019.

Information boards will be installed at the entrance to Bled, to direct traffic to free places in public car parks and there will be control panels from parks to the lake. and the introduction of a one-way traffic to Kolodvorska cesta, around Prešernova Cesta from the hotel Astoria to the Bledec hostel.

There are now 8 locations with public toilets in Bled

- Seliše (near the Mercator)
- Ice hall
- Shopping center
- Camp
- Tribune veslaške (viewing platforms at Velika Zaka)
- Castle swimming area
- Festival Hall

A quick word about language

Almost all Slovenians you will meet in Bled, Ljubljana or any of the main tourism towns speak or have a good understanding of English. Some younger people speak it as if it were their first language. They also often speak German and Italian (especially further north near Kranjska Gora), Croatian, and other Balkan languages.

English is often used as a "bridge" language by other European and Asian visitors.

Slovenians know that theirs is a difficult language. There are so many dialects even some Slovenians will not be understood throughout the country. Learn a few words of Slovenian. It will be appreciated. There are some suggestions as we go through the book.

Arriving in Bled

Most independent travellers arrive in Bled by car or bus, which is where I begin this book. We all carry mobile phones. Many of us are constantly connected to the internet where we can grab instant information, maps, directions and phone numbers. The aim of this book is to curate and present the information you need when you are in Bled or planning a visit; information which is practical and relevant to most visitors but will save you the research time on the web.

In this section, I want to keep the information as practical as possible for people arriving in the town for the first time.

The bulk of the book is written from experience. It tries to answer questions with that experience and sometimes inside knowledge.

- When you get off the bus as you arrive for the first time in Bled, do you go right or left to get to the lake? (It doesn't matter.)
- Where's the best cake shop? (It matters very much!)

- Where can I do my laundry? (For the sake of your fellow travellers!)□

Arriving by bus

Most people arriving by bus are travelling from Ljubljana or from the train station at Lesce where they pick up either a local service or join the bus from Ljubljana. Others come from the Bohinj direction going towards Ljubljana.

If you are arriving from Ljubljana or Lesce, Radovljica, Kranj direction, once the bus gets to the top of the hill just as you come into Bled, you will get your first sight of the town. It is more than likely that the first stop is not for you unless you are going to Hotel Krim, Union or some of the hostels and apartments nearby. You are more likely going to the Bled bus station (Avtobusna postaja Bled). Some first-time visitors scramble to get off here at Union stop. The drivers are used to it and will announce this is not where you want to be. Some first-time visitors ignore the driver; he knows what he's talking about, people.

When the bus pulls into the station a few minutes later (often 19 minutes past the hour), you get off at the back door. If there is a crowd – and at the height of the summer, there almost always is – there is usually confusion. Some people wanting to board the bus will demand tickets to Ljubljana (usually at 30 minutes past the hour) – this bus is not for Ljubljana, it is going on to Bohinj Jezero, Bohinj Zlatorog or that direction.

Slovenian bus destination boards can be befuddling on first sight. Until recently there were literally boards in the driver's wind-screen. Almost all are now digital displays, although a few boards are still to be seen.

The bus from Ljubljana to Bohinj Zlatorog will display "Ljubljana - Bohinj Zlatorog" and usually include Kranj' Naklo, Radolijca and Bled.

The first name on the display says where the bus has come from (Ljubljana) and the second, where it is going (Bohinj

Zlatorog). Below that, smaller letters naming some of the towns it passes through. This can cause bewilderment among new visitors which is often expressed simultaneously in many European and Asian languages.

The circumstances are compounded by co-incidences in the timetable. The Bohinj to Ljubljana bus arrives about the same time as the Ljubljana to Bohinj bus. As you get off, other people are milling about confused about getting on. Normally busses are keep to their timetables and are reliable, but with road works and extraordinary numbers of visitors in the summer, delays are understandable, but add to the confusion.

Of course, other destinations are served from Bled, so there could be two or three other busses arriving around the same time. Read the destination boards.

On a hot summer's day patience is strained. I really admire the bus drivers who just take it in their stride, talking to the passengers, sometimes in three or four languages.

When people arrive in Bled, they usually want one of these questions answered almost as soon as they get off the bus:

- Where is the cash machine?
- Where are the toilets?
- Where is the lake?
- Where is the coffee/beer/wine/cream cake?

Important words in Slovenian

Bled Cream Cake:

Blejska kremna rezina (often known as "Kremsnita")

There are detailed answers to those questions later on but here are a few quick replies to the frequently asked questions.

We will answer by taking a short walk from the bus to the Tourist Information Centre.

When you get off the bus it doesn't matter whether you turn left or right to get to the lake, either will do. If you go left at the bus, take the immediate right, if you go right take the immediate left.

Coffee/beer/wine/cream cake?

Thirty seconds walk from the bus and you are spoilt for choice.

Caffe Peglez'n is a small traditional place with a big terrace. It is favoured by locals as well as visitors and is one of my top three places for coffee and calm in Bled. It's on the right as you walk towards the lake.

Art Café is modern and attracts younger clientele including students from the two nearby colleges. A wide range of drinks is available, as are snacks and in the winter excellent hot chocolate.

Vinoteka Zdravljica is a few paces past the Art Café. It is stocked with about a hundred Slovenian wines. There is a dozen or so on the wine list to be bought by the glass. This place is a personal favourite. Sitting outside on a warm summer's day watching the world go by, reading a book, looking up at the castle, sipping Rebula or Malvazija - Slovenian white wines ... heaven.

You can read more about Art Café, Vinoteka Zdravljica and Caffe Peglez'n and the other cafes and restaurants in the area in the Food and Drinks section.

Important words in Slovenian

Cheers:
We say "Cheers" as a toast. Slovenians are more likely to say 'Na zdravie.' ("to health").
'Živijo.' is often used.

15

Where is the lake?

There it is; just past those cafés. And there is Bled Castle up on the hill. And there is St. Martin's Church, and the island, and the view, and the swans, and ducks.

Altogether, a great big helping of the Bled experience.

Dobrodošli na Bledu ... Welcome to Bled

Where are the toilets?

Usually marked, for your convenience (sorry) as WC or sometimes "Stranišča". As you would expect, the cafés and bars have toilets. From the bus station, the nearest public toilets are just past the Festival Hall (Festivalna dvorana) on the left just as you get to the horse drawn carriages (fijaker). You'll need a 50-cent coin or 10 and 20-cents to the value. There are other public toilets in the main Shopping Centre. By summer 2018 there will be eight public toilets in the town and around the lake.

If you only have bank notes, there is a change making machine at the carpark beside the shopping centre. There was one beside the fijaker, but no longer.

First time visitors to Slovenia often remark on how clean the country is. And it is. That cleanliness extends to the toilets. They are spotless, well maintained and safe.

Where is the Cash Machine, the ATM?

Walk on, toward the shopping area about 200 meters and you will see the Gorenjska banka ATM. he bank has moved but the cash machine remains. There is another machine at the shopping centre at the SKB.

Along the way, you will pass the beautiful town hall on the left. Once you have your cash, walk along a little further for the Park Hotel, the home of Bled cream cake, more coffee and one of the best views over the lake toward the castle.

Other questions

- **Where is Tourist Information?** After you leave the Gorenjska Bank cash machine (bankomat) continue to walk toward the Casino. There is a sign for tourist information to the right. You can get maps and books, gifts and advice. There is also bike and car hire here.

  Infocenter Triglavska roža is about a 10-minute walk away at Ljubljanska cesta 27. When you reach the Park Hotel (on your left) turn left and keep going. The Infocenter is on your left.

- **Where can I hire a car?** It will probably be less expensive if you can book a car before you arrive on the car hire website. There are several advantages to this. First you can compare prices (there are up to 6 agents in town), arrange to pick up from Bled and return to the same place or another rental office – there is usually no charge for that.

  Beware, though, of costs not obvious or you are not informed of right up front. I had used Eurocar for years. Last time in May 2018 I paid full insurance when I hired a small car. I scrapped two wheel covers during the hire – inexpensive to replace. No matter, insurance would cover that. Yet I was stung for £60 "administration". I will be checking "administration" costs next time I hire a car.

- **Where can I do my laundry?** The Speed Queen laundrette is near the bus station and close to most of the hostels and backpacker accommodation. It is new, cheap, fast, bright and clean. The whole process takes about an hour. Prešernova cesta 50, 4260 Bled. Phone +386 41 366323. (If you see Tomas the owner, say hello from me.)

- **Where's good for lunch?** There are lots of places to eat. In the food and drinks section I nominate the best places I have visited. There is a more exhaustive list if you want more information. If you are under pressure and just want a quick snack by the lake, then the Mercator in the shopping centre is the place to go to buy sandwiches, cheese, bread, fruit and drinks including wine and beer.

Leaving by bus

There are two main departure points; Bled Bus Station and Union stop on the main road the Ljubljana, away from the town. As mentioned in the "Arriving by Bus" section, things can become a little confusing during the summer as people from half a dozen different countries try to work out if this is the bus they want.

Bus destination display show (first) where the bus started its journey and the destination (second) with some other places between the two names. To add to the confusion at the station, buses going to Ljubljana and from Ljubljana arrive within minutes of each other. The other bus stop, opposite the Union restaurant is for Ljubljana. And finally, Bled bus station serves other destinations, nearby towns and villages. It can become quite busy.

Important words in Slovenian

Railway station:
Železniška postaja

Bus station:
Avtobusna postaja

When is the bus to Bohinj?
Kdaj je avtobus do Bohinja?

When is the bus to Ljubljana?
Kdaj je avtobus v Ljubljano?

Arriving by train

There are two train stations serving Bled, which is not the same as saying there are two train stations in Bled. There are not.

Bled Jezero railway station, which is on the line from Jesenice to Nova Gorica, is high above the north-western side of the lake. It is not well placed if you are going to the town or the hostel and hotel area. It is almost 3 kms from the town centre. The main camping ground is much closer – 10 minutes or so down a steep hill. Hotel Triglav is very close to the station.

The line continues to Nova Gorica on the Italian border. Services are infrequent, but it is a beautiful journey. It makes a lovely day out. Several times a year, an historic railway journey is played out from the station. See more about The Heritage Train in Part 7 of this book.

Insider Knowledge:

I have noticed people take the train service from Ljubljana to Jesenice and not get off at Bled-Lesce which it passes through. They change trains Jesenice in and then travel to Bled Jezero. That whole journey is about 3 hours. You might think it makes sense to you and your arrangements, particularly if you are going to the camp site.

Bled-Lesce railway station is 4 km from Bled. You can catch a bus to Bled (and other destinations) across the road from the railway station. The service from there is good and frequent during the day. However, in the evening and on Sundays there can be long gaps between buses. The journey is about 10 minutes stopping at Bled Union and Bled bus station. It takes about an hour to walk. I imagine you could rent or buy a bicycle from the large cycle shop near the station. When all other alternatives are exhausted, you can get a taxi. Taxis from Lesce to Bled are expensive. Be prepared to pay €15 for the ten-minute 4 km trip. The last time I took a taxi from Lesce to Mlino the charge on the meter was a few cents short of €20 (December 2016).

Arriving by car

Parking can be difficult. At the height of the summer 2017, there were stories of long tailbacks into the town from the highway, impossible to find parking space.

A long-awaited by-pass is currently under construction and should be ready in the early summer 2018. Until then Bled's through traffic to Bohinj and Pokljuka will remain heavy. There are also plans to build a new car and coach park close to the main entrance to Bled Castle. In 2018 there will be a coach park, and then develop into a coach and car park.

That should be in full operation in 2020 and will take a lot of pressure off the town's infrastructure.

As he drives me from the airport my friend Luka says, "We need a carpark here." We are just passing the entrance to the new Mercator. "People could park here are and walk to the lake or there could be a tourist train or shuttle." He is quite right. Bled needs more parking.

Personally, I would avoid arriving by car at the height of the summer, especially at the weekend. Until that new car park is available, it might even be worth parking in Lesce and taking the bus into Bled. This is not a recommendation, merely a suggestion from someone who has been stuck in a long tail of traffic on a hot summer day.

If you arrive by car you will probably come via one of three directions, the Ljubljana/Jesenice highway, from Bohinj or possibly from Vintgar Gorge. On a hot busy weekend, I wish you luck. There are lots of parking places, but they fill up quickly.

There is parking along cesta Svobode from around about the bus station and in front of Festival Hall. But that is more limited now. Don't rely on it. And it is not suitable for camper vans. The roads around here are too narrow, and people walk here.

There is more parking beside the Sports Stadium, behind Vila Prešeren, behind Hotel Krim and a few other places. If you can't find somewhere easily, I suggest going out of town – not toward Mlino, you have no chance there, but toward Ljubljana. Many of the parking places have limited time allowances; as little as 30 minutes, often 2 hours.

The two main petrol stations are on Ljubljanska cesta on the road towards the highway.

If you plan to visit Mlino, there is a large abandoned building just past Vila Bled. The space around it is used by tour coaches for parking. You might find some room there. But the time allowance is limited. The walk all the way back to the town centre is about 25 minutes. But what a walk. Breath taking.

Arriving by motorbike

You will see signs outside many of the bars and restaurants here in the Gorenjska region welcoming bikers. Touring bikers are often seen on the winding mountain roads. Harley Davidson clubs meet in Bled during the summer and thunder through the mountain roads nearby. The information for bikers is the same as everyone else, but you might want to prioritise places where bikers are particularly welcome. You have a better chance of meeting likeminded people and get advice and suggestions for your visit.

You are here!

Now you have arrived and dealt with personal needs like laundry, cash, coffee, and cake, you can start exploring.

Getting around

Bike hire is the most common way to get around (after walking of course). They can be hired by the hour, half day or day. It takes 30 to 45 minutes to whizz around the lake on a bike, so if you are pressed for time, that could be one solution.

There is a variety of bikes to choose from, and process vary, but this is a competitive service and the pricing is pretty good.

Around the bus station there are several shops with rides available.

You can also hire long-boards, scooters and the most recent addition is e-Bikes. If you want something more adventurous try an e-bike tour. More information at www.ebiketour.si.

Tourist Train costs €5 and takes around the lake in about 25 minutes. You can hop on and hop off only once.

Horse drawn carriage will cost €50, but up to 4 people can travel together. You will find the coachmen (fijaker) beside Festival Hall.

The Hop On – Hop Off Bus

This is an excellent – and environmentally friendly – way to get around the towns and villages nearby. The Slovenian Alps and Gorenjska area are places of outstanding natural beauty and Slovenia works hard to be a "green" country. The bus is just one way to protect the environment.

During July and August 2018 there are four departures from Bled each day starting at 9:30 except Thursday when there are five departures. Some stops include additional tours and visits which are priced separately. There are also some free tours. There are some great places to stop and have lunch – Kropa and Begunje in Gorenjska

Tuesday's tour includes Radovljica, with its tiny, beautiful old town centre has several museums and bourgeois houses. The tour also passes by the villages Posavec and Ljubno and visits the historic Kropa with the iron forging heritage sits in a valley with the river Kroparice thundering through it. I recommend the free guided tours every Tuesday at 10.30 and 12.30.

Wednesdays are Bee Tour days on the HO/HO bus in 2018. First to Selo pri Bledu then on to Lesce's modern beekeeping centre. The tour continues to Žirovnica and Breznica then back to Radovljica and its Museum of Apiculture.

Thursday tours visit the historic villages near Bled including Vrba the birthplace of Slovenia's greatest poet Prešeren.

Žirovnica, Begunje na Gorenjskem, and Brezje the largest Slovene Pilgrimage Centre.

On Friday Begunje na Gorenjskem check out the Avsenik museum then a spectacular drive to the old craft town Tržič. Visit the museum and wander around the ancient streets and paths. Look hard, you might find "Paradise". But not as you might have expected it.

A full day ticket is €8, children under 10 travel free. More info and timetables at:

https://www.radolca.si/sl/aktivnosti/hop-on-hop-off-bus

TIC Radovljica, Linhartov trg 9, Radovljica Phone: + 386 4531 5112. info@radolca.si

The Island
There are 321 bodies of water in Slovenia classified as lakes. There is only one lake island. There are river islands, an underground lake island and constructed islands, but the island in Lake Bled is unique.

Getting to and from

Pletna: The traditional way to visit the island is by pletna, a flat-bottomed boat with a colourful canopy rowed by a pletnar standing at the stern. The design of these boats is unique to Bled. The cost is €14 for adults and €7 for children. However, your time on the island is limited to 40 minutes, and you return with the same pletnar. The journey lasts between 10 and 20 minutes each way depending on your point of departure.

There are several pletna piers around the lake. Probably best to start with the pier behind the Park Hotel where there are usually two pletna in constant use. The pletnar will decide the time of departure when there are enough passengers. There is a larger pletna pier in Mlino, but it is more usually used for organised trips.

Hydrobus also leaves from the same pier on the hour 10:00, 11:00, 12:00, 14:00, 15:00, 16:00, 17:00, 18:00. Adults pay €11, children €6. You should talk to the operator about how long you can stay on the island.

Rowing Boat: There are a few places to rent a boat around Mlino and the Camping Site at Zaka. The main advantage here is not only price per person, but the time you spend on the island is your choice. Boat hire is usually about 2 hours.

Swim: Yes, you can swim there, but you cannot go on the island wearing a swimming suit.

The story

There are many legends and stories about the island, but I'll keep to a few facts here. The Church of the Mother of God on the Lake is the beautiful building sitting on the island – it is surprising how many pictures online call it Bled Castle (which is at the top of the cliff). The first church established there was in 1465 more than 400 years after the establishment of the Castle. Inside there are several small side chapels, reclaimed artefacts and of course the Wishing Bell. Pull the rope, ring the bell, make a wish.

You can also climb the renovated clock tower, after climbing the 99 steps to get up to the church, but souvenirs and coffee. It is a place of pilgrimage. It has been regarded over the centuries (including pre-Christian times) as a holy place. That seems too often to get lost in the tourism and commerce. With luck and patience, you will find a quiet corner if that is what you are looking for, to take a moment's reflection.

There is more about the island, its stories and pletnar late in this book.

Where to get information when you arrive in Bled - Tourist Information
The Tourist Information Centre is in the main shopping area beside the Casino. The staff are very friendly and knowledgeable. They will have information about what is going on in Bled and the surrounding area. They will usually

help you with other questions about Slovenia. You can also hire a bike or car (Hertz).

Turistično društvo Bled, cesta Svobode 10 4260 Bled. Phone: +386 (0)4 5741 122

Opening Times: Mon - Sat: 8:00 am - 7:00 pm Sun: 10:00 am - 4:00 pm

If you are a serious walker, hiker, cyclist, climber or adventure tourist/traveller and plan to explore the Triglav National Park, the first stop should be

Infocenter Triglavska roža Bled Ljubljanska cesta 27, SI - 4260 Bled. Phone: +386 (0)4 5780 205

E-mails:

- Bled: info@dzt.bled.si,
- Slovenian Alps: info@slovenian-alps.com,
- Triglav National Park: info.trb@tnp.gov.si

Opening times: Spring and Summer, every day from 8.00 am to 6.00 pm. Rest of the year every day from 8.00 am to 4.00 pm.

There is a permanent exhibition about the Triglav National Park, a book and souvenir shop, and a nice little café. If it is a rainy day and you want to spend an hour pottering around, looking at gifts to bring home or just kill time, this is a good place to visit.

Shopping for fun and survival

There are two reasons to shop; because you need something and because you want something. Sometimes you just want to shop. Food and day to day shopping are straight forward. There are several supermarket chains in Slovenia; Mercator, Tuš, Spar, Hoffer and Lidl among them.

Shopping for survival and groceries

There are four or five Mercator in Bled. The biggest is Supermarket Bled at Kajuhova cesta 1. It opened in March 2017 and is great for a big family shop. There is a mid-sized Mercator in the main shopping centre which is handy if you want to pick up something for a picnic beside the lake. There are convenience Mercators at Campsite Zaka and at Mlino. There is another at Prešernova cesta 48, 4260 Bled, Slovenia beside the Speed Queen laundrette which is close to the main hostels.

The opening times of the smaller shops depend on the season and the Mercator at the campsite is closed in the winter. As a rough guide, they are open by 8:00 am and closed by 6:00 pm Monday to Friday. Weekend opening hours are more limited. In the winter, for example Mlino is closed on Sundays. Opening times are displayed at the entrance.

The nearest Tuš is in Lesce where you will also find Spar (Alpska cesta 34). Lidl and Hofer are out of town at Hraška cesta 22.

Insider Knowledge:

When you are buying loose fruit and vegetables in the supermarket, after bagging what you want WEIGH THEM and get a PRICE STICKER before going to the checkout desk. That info was so important I used capitals.

Shopping for fun
Huberto Široka is probably the best-known jeweller in Bled. His workshop is just opposite the Grand Hotel Toplice.

Huberto was born in Zagreb in 1960 but spent his childhood in Paris and Bled. He started his career as a goldsmith at the age of 24. In 1990, he officially became an International Master of Fine Arts and decided to become an "independent culture worker" as he puts it. He has exhibited throughout Slovenia and further afield.

Much of his work is inspired by what he sees and experiences around the town, the lake and the surrounding area. He says, "There is a lot of Bled's history in my work, which I'm trying to maintain and add to with inspiration from the present-day. Years ago, I made one of the most beautiful archaeological finds "Peacock – bird of Eden". It is a symbol of Bled and brings people laughter and happiness. Happiness comes when people laugh." The peacock symbol is to be seen around Bled and is an important figure in Huberto's work.

"The path around the lake is the source of my inspiration in all seasons - summer, autumn, winter, spring - when the rain or snow is falling, when the sun is shining, all times of the day or night, it always brings me calmness."

There is a short video of Huberto at work on Bled.tv [*www.bled.tv/huberto-siroka-glas-mojstra-ob-jezeru*]

Huberto's workshop is at cesta Svobode 19 Bled.
Phone: +386 (0)40 22 68 05

Near the Park Hotel these are many places to buy Slovenian souvenirs. One you might just miss but should visit is Mikame just beside the Devil Bar. "Mikame means I could be tempted." Says Jakob Ribnaker the young owner of the business. Although I think he might be pulling my leg. I can't find that translation. Enthusiastic, effervescent as only young people can be, and fluent in English, Jakob sells pottery made by his mother who lives in Bled. Quirky eccentric pottery, each piece unique decorated with childlike illustrations of birds and frogs. Vibrant colours, striking design. There are tulip shaped mugs on the shelf above with warm orange tones and bright flowers made by a neighbour. All the craft is Slovenian; much made nearby.

As part of the book there will be a series of podcasts and you can hear Jacob describe the gallery and crafts shop. Check www.davysims.com/bled-stories/

Cesta svobode 15, Bled, Slovenia
Phone +386 40 686 864

Markets

The Arts and Crafts Fair on cesta Svobode near the Festival Hall is open every Friday, Saturday and Sunday from 10:00 am to 7:00 pm from Spring to Autumn. It features work by Slovenian crafts people and artists who staff the stalls themselves and are very happy to discuss what's on offer.

The Triglav Market is held every third Saturday in the month at the Information Centre, Triglavska roža Bled. It is open between 10:00 am and 12:00 noon.

Occasionally, food markets pop up during the summer. The Italian market was a real treat for the eye and the taste buds.

Some farms are open to visitors during the year. **Homestead pr'Dornk** is one. The 240-year-old building is in Mlino, 200 meters from the lake (follow the sign to Selo). They produce their own brandy, schnapps, beer and traditional food. They say that their Farmer snack is among their most popular. It is cold cut with a smoked minced bacon (Slovenian name is zaseka), dry sausage, prosciutto, domestic salami and cheese, and homemade bread. You might have to book ahead depending on the time of the year. There is more information on their website [dornk-bled.com/home].

In the centre of the town there are two principle shopping areas. One is mainly tourist shopping. It is in the shadow of the Park Hotel, the other is the Shopping Centre opposite which you can't miss – even if you wanted to.

Trgovski Centre (or just, The Shopping Centre)
The shopping centre is known locally as the Gadafi Centre. They say that the explanation as to why such an extraordinary structure is found on the shore of one of the prettiest places in the world is that it was originally intended for Libya. No-one has yet been able to explain to me why or how it was built in Bled rather than Tripoli. However, researching for this book I have found that the website for the shopping centre [*www.shoping.si* that's "shoping" with

one "p"] titles its homepage "Domov Gadafi" and "Gadafi" is a search term on the website. Perhaps it is more than a nickname.

There are around sixty outlets on four floors set around a main piazza where you can sit out in the sun – shaded by big umbrellas – and order coffee, snacks and drinks. Which café will serve you will depend on where you sit. There are other bars, cafés and restaurants around the centre, but this is a great spot for simple coffee, snacks and people watching.

You will also find clothes shops, sports shops, a tiny wine shop stocked with Slovenian wines. It is an open sunny and relaxed spot where you can sip drinks and top up your tan or find cooler corners under shade.

Often in the summer, it becomes one of the town's concert venues, especially for the Golden Microphone competition. More about that and other music events elsewhere in this book.

Even if you are in Bled for a short time, have a quick look around. You might be able to buy everything you need here in one visit, then go on to enjoy what you came here to do.

Money

Slovenia is in the Euro-zone. As a country, it has a reputation for being comparatively inexpensive. Bled and Ljubljana are more expensive than other parts of Slovenia, but costs are pretty good. Although they have been creeping up in recent years. I will mention some in the reviews.

Insider Knowledge:

Try to have change in your purse or pocket. I really don't know why, but the shops are always looking for exact change. This is not unique to Bled. Finding the right coins is almost a national sport. This is not helped by the ATMs that insist on spitting out €50 notes which are often held in contempt in some shops if you are making a small purchase.

Banks

The two most easily found banks are Gorenjska Banka branch office which has moved from the Park Hotel building to the new Mercator shopping centre. Kajuhova cesta 1 with new opening hours, Monday to Friday: 8:00 to 19:00 Saturday, 08:00 to 12:30 and closed Sunday.

SKB Banka in the Gadafi shopping centre is much less convenient time-wise. It is open Monday to Friday 8:30 to 12:00 and 14:00 to 17:00, Saturdays and Sundays closed. But don't take that €50 note to the bank teller and ask for it to be changed - there will be a charge.

You are now prepared with just about everything you need to know before you arrive. Let's decide when is best to go.

PART 2 –
BEST TIMES TO VISIT

There is always something to bring you back to Bled. During each season you will discover something to attract you. In winter (zima) 2011 and January 2017 the lake froze. People were skating, playing ice-hockey walking to the island. The pletna boats we out of the water. In the autumn/fall (jesen), the rich red and brown colours appear on the trees around the lake. The spring and summer (pomlad, poletje) are a festival of sport, arts and music.

Whether it is winter skiing in Gorenjska, summer concerts, the rowing and running, the Winter Fairy-tale (Advent and Christmas fair), Bled changes with the seasons.

Spring (March, April, May)

Once the Christmas tree is taken down and the Winter Fairy-tale packs up for another year, the town becomes very quiet. There are still some winter activities – the ice-rink is open in the Park Hotel terrace. There are some events and sports at Straža. If there is snow and it is good enough, there will be skiing there. There is skiing in Pokljuka the annual biathlon is scheduled for the end of January and beginning of February. The town accepts that it is time for a communal winter snooze.

Before Easter

Easter in 2018 was on 1 April. In 2019 it will be 21 April.

In Rio they have Mardi Gras, some of us have Shrove Tuesday. Around the Christian world there are celebrations and preparations for Lent. In Slovenia on the eve of this traditional religious observance, there are parades and costume extravaganzas. This carnival season tends towards welcoming the spring and scaring away the old year. Parades are held in many towns in Slovenia including Bled where up to 20 groups from the community dressed in costume and fancy dress, parade through the streets – and the snow – on the Sunday before Lent.

The most famous parade in Slovenia is the Kurentovanje celebration in Ptuj – about 200 km from Bled. Here the magnificently costumed Kurents parade through the town chasing away winter by jumping and making noise. Tradition has it that they bring spring and abundance to the land. The unmistakable shaggy outfits consist of a hat, a sheep-skin suit, green or red knee-high stockings, bells attached to a chain around the belt, and a ježevka (a thick stick with hedgehog spines). The door-to-door rounds of the Kurent are on the UNESCO List of Intangible Cultural Heritage of Humanity.

Škoromati are the oldest Carnival masks in Slovenia. On Shrove Saturday, you can find them in the villages of the southern slopes of the Brkini Hills and the Podgrajsko-Matarsko Plain in the south west of the country. Here the costumed characters go door-to-door rounds collecting gifts from people's homes on a "Poberija".

The Laufarija festival in Cerkno (about 60 km from Bled). Ljubljana holds the Dragon Carnival, where a large green dragon leads the parade. There is an Istrian Carnival on the coast. A large carnival at the central square in Maribor. And in nearby old town centre of Kranj, you can join in the Prešeren Carnival.

Back in Bled, there are events, in March and April, but fewer. Some take place each year, so for 2018, read also 2019.

In 2018 in March:

- the 57th FIS Ski World Cup Vitranc in Kranjska Gora (3 and 4 March)

- the 28th Pokljuka cross country ski marathon and half marathon held on the courses of the Sports Centre Triglav Pokljuka in Rudno polje (3 March)
- People staying in Bled can take special bus connections to the main ski resorts; Vogel, Krvavec, Kranjska Gora, Cerkno and 3ländereck as well as the less demanding slopes in Pokljuka.
- The Bled Water Festival is held at the Festival Hall, in late March

Easter

The sound of a big brass band heralds the beginning of spring and the Easter celebrations bring the town – and the tourists – back to life. In 2018 Easter is on 1 April. If you are planning beyond this year, in 2019 Easter celebrations will be a little later in the month, 19 April.

The traditionally liveried Godba Gorje brass band plays at every significant occasion in Bled and the nearby villages. The Municipality of Gorje is about 5 km from Bled, but many of the musicians are from the town. It has represented Slovenia around the world over the decades. They look impressive and the sound they make is the sound of Gorenjska. The Easter activities and the season have begun.

It is no exaggeration to say that Bled is a sunny place. The sun shines year-round and while there are sometimes torrential showers, and rain lasting for days on end, even in the summer, you are more likely to experience a sunny day any time of the year. Spring brings cool days and evenings. From spring through to the summer, you might experience night time thunder and lightning as storms roll in from neighbouring Italy or Austria.

The first annual regatta is held at the end of April; in 2018 on 21 and 22 the **59th May Day Rowing Regatta**.

In May (this year on 18th to 20th) the **Accordion Festival** comes to town. It began in 2013 and it is an event worth making the trip to see. Accordionists, accordion clubs, professional musicians, learners, amateurs and lovers of the sound descend on Bled and spend at least a day playing all over the town.

It is one of the most joyful events of the year. The climax is when all the musicians line the lake shore in Spa Park to play one song together, Slavko Avsenik – "Otocek sredi jezera" (Island in the middle of the lake). It is a wonderful experience. If you have missed it already you should keep an eye out for next year. Search YouTube for "Main Accordion Performance" and "400 Accordions" to see how they performed in 2014 and 2015.

From the end of May, schools and colleges throughout Europe release their students into the world. They buy Interrail tickets and before too long arrive in Bled finding beds in town's hostels.

At this time the weather is fresh and cool and bright and sunny. But there is not a lot of organised entertainment. This is the time to use Bled as a base and explore Gorenjska, the nearby villages and towns. Time to hike and sail, to cycle, to enjoy the rivers making their way down from the Alps.

At the end of May, the competitive rowing season begins, and young athletes are active on the lake. This is a centre for the Slovenian national rowing team.

Summer (June, July, August)

It can be hot. During this period friends who are long-time residents report that they have experienced temperatures of up to 40C at the beginning of the summer. I have enjoyed 35C for more than 10 consecutive days in July and August. There is no guarantee there won't be rain, but it is unlikely. In June, the restaurants and bars that have been closed for the winter open their doors and tables appear outside.

Events become more frequent. Bled Castle has been open all winter, but at the beginning of June (2nd and 3rd June 2018), the Medieval Days campsite sets up outside the walls of the castle. (See Bled Castle Events)

Events climax with the music and sporting festivals that dominate the summer. The restaurants and bars are at their best, the days are long, and the nights are hot. People are extremely well behaved. Spirits are high but there is little or no public drunkenness, no public misbehaviour at all. You will feel (and are) safe. The buses are full, the roads are busy and at times the town gets choked. If you are not planning a long stay in Bled, aim for mid-week during July and August. Although some of the best events are at the weekend.

I like to disappear on Saturday and Sunday afternoons. This is the time the weekenders and day trippers arrive by bus, by car, by motorbike. Families from other parts of Slovenia or Italy or Austria fill the streets and the lakeshore.

Yet within a few minutes you can escape to a quiet place away from the lake. It is easy to find walks in places where the buzz of the holiday centre is replaced by the buzz of insects. Cycle to Selo or Bodešče or Ribno. Walk to Kupljenik – get advice about where you can get the most spectacular views there.

If you want to escape into the mountains, first visit the Infocenter Triglavska roža for advice about safe walks, maps and any other serious walking kit.

For motorists there is no Bled bypass although planning permission was granted in March 2017 and work should be completed by the busiest time in 2018. Until it opens, the road through the town is also the route to other tourist centres like Lake Bohinj or Triglav National Park. Late on a Sunday evening in the dusk you will see cars snaking around the lake going back who knows how far making their way back whence they came.

Autumn (September, October, November)

The colours around the lake change – it is spectacular. From about mid-August you can feel a change. As the church bells peal around the town and nearby villages on 15 August for the feast of the Assumption, you may feel a slight difference in temperature. There is a pleasant breeze and the evenings are cooler.

And in the early mornings there are more photographers around the lake capturing the new colours emerging from the green hillsides. By the end of November some of the mountain peaks in the distance begin to turn white. The early morning mists are pink and orange in the sunrise. The "blue hour" is in the evening.

There are still activities around the town, but fewer and some places begin to close. There are not as many tourists and significantly fewer day trippers. Even though the tour buses still come and expel their exhausts into the clean Alpine air, this is my favourite time of the year.

Winter (December January February)

In 2017 Bled was ranked in the top 10 most popular winter destinations for Instagram lovers. As 2016 ended on New Year's Eve, the town partied in sub-zero temperatures, under the Christmas lights. Within the first few days of 2017, the pletna boats had been pulled from the water as the lake froze, the first time since 2011. For most of January the lake became a play space and people walked to the island. The surrounding mountains white against a clear blue sky.

A white winter cannot be guaranteed, although 2017 ended with more snow. Even well into February 2018 there were still many days of skiing on Straža.

December arrives as does the Christmas market "Winter Fairy-tale". Since 2015, Bled has set up a market near the shore of the lake with entertainment every evening and highlights during the month. You can see the tall Christmas tree covered in white lights from all around the lake. Musicians perform on the stage every night. Fires and blankets keep you warm. The festival goers share the trellis tables where they eat hot food from the stalls operated by the town's restaurants. They drink beer and mulled wine (kuhano vino), and schnapps and hot chocolate (vroča čokolada).

On the evening of the 30th December, one big community event brings locals from their homes and tourists from their hotels. They meet all around the lake and attempt a "Circle of Friendship". Stewards direct the crowds of people into tidy lines. We all hold glowsticks and hold hands.

There is a party on New Year's Eve when temperatures can be minus 10C or lower. Fireworks mark the end of the old year and the beginning of the new. And we sing, and we dance, and we cheer, and we wish everyone "srečno novo leto".

And we enter a new year.

Slovenian Cultural Holiday on 8 February 2019 will mark 170 years since the death of France Prešeren who is regarded as one of Slovenia's greatest poets. He is the most revered and is a symbol of Slovenia's nationhood. A verse from his poem A Toast is used in the Slovenian National Anthem.

In the original

> Žive naj vsi narodi
> Ki hrepene dočakat' dan
> Da koder sonce hodi
> Prepir iz sveta bo pregnan
> Da rojak
> Prost bo vsak
> Ne vrag, le sosed bo mejak!

The official Translation

> God's blessing on all nations
> Who long and work for that bright day
> When o'er earth's habitations
> No war, no strife shall hold its sway
> Who long to see
> That all men free
> No more shall foes, but neighbours be!

37

(Translation by Janko Lavrin)

He wrote about Bled in The Baptism at The Savica and lived in nearby Vrba. There is information about Prešeren scattered throughout this book, but if you want to explore his life and times, visit Kranj where he worked.

Skiing is the main sport at this time of the year. Both Vogel and Kravavec are each about an hour from Bled and special buses leave Bled in the morning returning in the evening during the winter ski season.

Through January and February there are some water sports events around the lake and in Pokljuka skiing any events.

Time to take a moment to reflect, a glass with a friend and in no time at all the party begins all over again.

Important words in Slovenian

Beer: Pivo
One beer, please: Eno pivo Prosim

Two beers, please: Dve pivi Prosim
Three/four/five beers please:
Tri/štiri/pet piva prosim

Wine: Vino

Bicycle: Kolo
 (Rowing) boat: (Veslanje) čoln

Money: Denar
How much does that cost?
Koliko stane?

PART 3 – EVENTS THROUGHOUT THE YEAR

Music

People come to Bled all year round, but the busiest time is, unsurprisingly, the summer. It is also the time when the town is most active. Sports events and music dominate, but there are many other cultural occasions, too.

Three music highlights combine around July and August and together provide the most exciting and exhilarating part of the year. They are Festival Bled, Okarina Festival and Bled Days and Bled Nights. If you are very lucky and can spend a lengthy period in Bled, you will remember this time for years to come.

The Accordion Festival which began in 2013, is held in May, in 2018, on 20th at the Lakeside Promenade. Accordionists, accordion clubs, professional musicians, learners, amateurs and lovers of the sound all descend on Bled and spend at least a day playing all around the town.

It is one of the most joyful events of the year. The climax is when all the musicians line the lake shore in Spa Park to play one song together, Slavko Avsenik's – "Otocek sredi jezera" (Island in the middle of the lake). It is Bled's own anthem.

They all play in the same key (well, most of them), but the speed seems to be entirely at the discretion of each group. It is a wonderful experience. 6th Meeting of Accordionists by Lake Bled in 2018 will be on 20 May at Lakeside Promenade. If you have missed it already you should keep an eye out for next year. It's worth a trip to see.

Search YouTube for "Main Accordion Performance" and "400 Accordions" to see how they performed in 2014 and 2015.

Slavko Avsenik

Slavko Avsenik is a cultural icon in Slovenia. His "Oberkrainer" music – largely polka – defined the country music from this region. His influence travelled far into Croatia, Austria, northern Italy, Switzerland and beyond. There is a multitude (hundreds even thousands) of bands playing his and similar music in Slovenia and beyond. A typical band will be dressed in traditional Gorenjska outfits, and the instrument line-up will be guitar, bass, drums, along with the two most important instruments, an accordion and a tuba, along with a male and a female singer. The accordionist more often than not plays the lead role, like a guitarist in a rock band.

A festival of Oberkrainer music is held in nearby Begunje na Gorenjskem, Avsenik's home village. It does not appear to be an annual event. The next is likely to be in 2019. More details here [festival.avsenik.com/en/]

In Bled the winter Oberkrainer festival "The Folk Music Hit Parade" is held on 10 November 2018 and other smaller events are held throughout the year.

Festival Bled
23rd Festival Bled 2 – 14 July

This classical music event features extraordinarily talented young musicians from around the world, most of whom are studying in the region. There is usually a jazz to the festival which was founded and is led by internationally known violinist and native of Bled, Jernej Brence. The classical masterclass are led by violinist Michael Frischenschlager.

The concerts are not just for serious music aficionados. The music is very accessible and often the concerts are by ensembles and musicians playing in a unique and entertaining way. If nothing else, should you be in Bled and the jazz music concert with the young musicians is on at the same time, do not miss it.

For up-to-date information on the Festival including concerts and venues. visit the website [*www.festivalbled.com/*]. For news of events and people participating search "Festival Bled" on Facebook.

Insider Knowledge

"This is my first tip. During Festival Bled, take a nice walk to Grand Hotel Toplice for a concert of young musicians and then, if you are in the mood, walk to Villa Prešeren for a drink on terrace by the lake.

"Or, for early morning, from Jarše, on the way to village Ribno, along the paths in the fields, walking, running or cycling to Dobra gora - a little hill next to Straža - and try yoga or just sit on a bench and admire the landscape."

Mojca Polajnar Peternelj

Okarina Festival

This celebration of world and Slovenian music begins just as Festival Bled ends. Sometimes they overlap a little. The two festivals are celebrations of music and share some of the same venues – Festival Hall and Bled Castle – but they are very different. For Okarina, a stage is built on the Promenade giving the audience incredible views of the musicians and mountains in the background as the sun sets. Musicians from around the world come to play in this unique setting. The 28th Okarina Festival will be held from July 26 to August 5, 2018, each evening at 8:30 pm at both Bled Castle and Promenade.

The line-up, as known just now is:

Venue: Bled Castle
25 July 8:30 pm   Dimitris Mystakidis, Greece

26 July 8:30 pm Waldemar Bastos, Angola

Venue: Promenade Bled
28 July 8:30 pm Gato Preto, Mozambique
29 July 8:30 pm Bokante, Guadalupe, USA
30 July 8:30 pm Deluxe, France
31 July 8:30 pm Los Mirlos, Peru
1 August 8:30 pm Dakh Daughters, Ukraine
2 August 8:30 pm Richard Thompson, UK
3 August 5:00 pm Yip's Children's Choir, Hong Kong and
 8:30 pm Fanfare Chokarlia, Romania
4 August 8:30 pm Guillaume Perret, France
5 August 8:30 pm Natacha Atlas, Egypt, UK

For news of the line-up and details of venues plus profiles of the artists, visit the festival website [*www.festival-okarina.si/en*].

Golden Microphone
This is another international festival of talented singers.
While it is open to all ages, it predominately features children and young people. In 2018. it will be held between 18 and 23 July. [*bled-goldenmic.si/en/*]

Folk Music Hit Parade

This celebration of Oberkrainer (Highland) music will be held in the Sport Hall, the biggest venue in the town. Around 2,000 people will be there to dance and sing along with Oberkrainer bands – traditional and folk music of the Alps. Slovenia, Austria, Bavaria, Switzerland, are usually all represented on stage and in the audience.

In 2018, it will be held on 10 November at 8:00 pm. It is an energetic, exciting celebration of a music style that developed in this area and based on the tradition of Alpine folk music, modernised and electrified. Book tickets in advance through Bled Tourism's website *www.bled.si/en/*

Guest DJs and Clubs throughout the summer play dance music inside and out. One of the most popular places in Kult

Klub, Ljubljanska cesta 4. There are updates on their Facebook page [*www.facebook.com/KultBled*].

For more information about events in Bled, the tourist board have a very good website at [*www.bled.si/en*].

Conferences

Some conferences return each year to Bled. The town hosts an annual Water Festival. The organisers say that the main purpose of the project is to raise public awareness about water issues in Slovenia, as well as in other parts of the world, provide solutions and work on its development. (15 June 2018)

Bled Strategic Forum

This is one of the most important political and social events of the year in this region. The Bled Strategic Forum attracts leading politicians from the western Balkans region, and ambassadors from around the world. Business people, journalists, political observers and activists are on the exclusive guest list. Between speeches, late night meetings and discussions, they mingle with prime ministers and foreign ministers.

In 2017 more than 1000 participants from 66 countries took part they engaged in more than 50 hours of sessions on pressing regional and global issues including human rights, digital diplomacy, environment and EU enlargement.

The Bled Strategic Forum will be held in September 2018. There is more information at [*www.bledstrategicforum.org/*]

PEN

Each spring, the PEN Writers' Meeting is held in Bled. 2018 see the 50th of these literary events. (17th to 22 April). Writers from around the world will be there to enjoy the literary festival.

Insider Knowledge

If you want to get a taste of this beautiful Gorenjska region there are some events held near Bled that are designed for local people rather than tourists.

One I heartily recommend is the St. Margaret's Fair at Bohinjska Bela. The 2018 date is 15 July. It lasts all day, but in the early evening, go looking for the local musicians playing music from the region, barbeques, beers, and dancing in the big tents.

Get directions from Bled Tourism. You can bus and walk or take a taxi to a truly community event.

Sports Events

Two years ago, Bled was winner in the Sports Destination category at the World Tourism Awards in London. Summer is the main sports season in the town, but some winter and ice sports also feature, not the least being ice hockey and skiing. Son of Bled, Anze Kopitar, plays for the US hockey team, the LA Kings. He is a local hero and many young players see him as a role model. Naturally, most of the sport goes on in or around the lake and in the Sports Hall (Športna dvorana).

Rowing – Bled has been a sports and health destination for over 100 years. Rowing championships are held, and there is a fantastic rowing centre on the lake (Župančičeva cesta 9, Phone: +386 (0)4 5767 230 email: info@vesl-klub-bled.si [*www.en.vesl-klub-bled.si/*]).

Check the rowing centre and bled.si websites for up to date information.

In the winter Bled is the centre for biathlons.

Chess has been a feature of the sports calendar since 1930. The World Senior Chess Championship will be held from 17 – 30 November.

Bled Triathlon is held at the Rowing Centre, Mala Zaka on 1 September 2018.

Cycling is a competitive sport, it is also the most convenient way to get around Bled. Cycle hire is widely available. However, people staying at least two months could buy a bike in Lesce and sell it back when they move on (just a suggestion).

The Bled Bike Festival is the leading and largest bike festival in Slovenia with competitors facing some of the toughest mountain routes. It will take place in Bled earlier in 2018 than last year, between 22nd and 24th June 2018. [*www.bledbikefestival.com* is the official website]

The 10k Night Run will be on 4 July 2017. The largest run of the year is around Lake Bled and is open to registered competitors. Keep up with developments and register at the website [*www.nocna10ka.net/eng*].

A more social and less competitive event is Bollé Original Lake Bled Run held in August.

Walking. Is it a sport? Is it a therapy? Is it a cultural or community event? Arnold Rikli brought health tourism to Bled over a hundred years ago, and now once a year an early morning walk is held in his honour. The 19th Rikli's Walk to Straža hill will be at 7:00 am on 1 July 2018 meeting in front of Hotel Golf.

Walking and hiking are popular and a serious business in Bled and in the whole region. If you are planning a walking holiday contact the Infocenter Triglavska roža Bled Ljubljanska cesta 27, Phone: +386 (0)4 5780 205

Fishing goes on all year round. You will need to purchase a licence. Find out the details of licence fees and regulations for the lake and for the nearby Sava Bohinjka and Radovna rivers at Fauna Slovenia Fly Fishing, cesta Svobode 12, Phone: 00386 41 633 147. [*www.faunabled.com*]). If you are already in town you will find the shop opposite the bus station.

There are more detailed rules and regulations at this website: [*www.ribiska-druzina-bled.si/price-list/?lang=en*]

Any other sports?
Well, you could try: Alpine and sport climbing, Ballooning, Bellyak, Geocaching, Golf, Hydrospeed, Sky Diving,

Horseback riding, Caving, Cycling, Kayaking, Mini golf, Motorcycling, Beach volley, Paintball and Airsoft, Summer tobogganing, Diving, Hiking, Rafting, Canyoning, Walks, Tennis and squash, Tubing,

Boating, Zipline, Alpine Skiing & Snowboarding, Biathlon, Ice climbing, Sledding, Cross-country skiing, Ski Touring, Snowshoeing which are all suggestions from the Bled Tourism website.

Four adventure shops and agents in Bled:

- Rafting Bled, Grajska cesta 4, 4260 Bled. Phone: +386 51 399 164 [tinaraft.si],
- 3glav Adventures, Ljubljanska cesta 1, 4260 Bled. Phone: +386 41 683 184 [3glav.com]
- Mamut Slovenia, cesta Svobode 4a, 4260 Bled. Phone: +386 40 121 900
- LIFE Events and Ribit gift shop, Grajska cesta 10, 4260 Bled Phone: +386 4 20 14 875 info@lifeevents.si

Insider Knowledge:

"I am not the cyclist I once was, but I still like to get away from the centre of Bled at times. Tourists are very welcome, but it's good to avoid them sometimes.

I cycle out from the centre on Ljubljanska cesta. Turn right and follow the signs to Koritno - about 5km. Sometimes I turn here and follow the sign back to Selo. Other times I will cycle on to Bodešče and cross the Sava before returning.

There are lots of paths and roads to explore here and you are only a few kilometres from Bled. I always bring a phone, water and something to eat. Maybe spend the whole day exploring. In the summer - drink plenty of water. It can get very hot and there is not a lot of shade in places. Joško

Bled Castle
Although Bled Castle organises events throughout the year independent of the town's tourism events, it is very much

part of the community. The castle is open every day for tours and visits, it also has an outstanding restaurant and spectacular views of the lake and surrounding area.

Among the attractions are the historical re-enactments. During the summer there are historic theatrical presentations twice a week. Halloween is celebrated with eerie events, dances and "frightening" (no – really, more fun than frightening) characters. The medieval camp at the beginning of the summer is a marvellous family experience.

A training camp is set up in the spring to exhibit archery, swordsmanship and other knights' skills. Costumed participants play early music, serve beer and food. There is the smell of wood burning and the sight of experts in medieval arts and military skills create an authentic atmosphere.

As you can imagine, children love swordfights between medieval knights and then they hold the swords themselves and mock fight with the same knights.

Inside this thousand-year-old building there is a state-of-the-art audio-visual exhibition of the Bled Castle history and the story of the surrounding area.

Historically this was a defensive and administrative castle rather than the home of kings and princesses but don't let that limit your imagination. Visitors will find lords and nobles, monks, printers and castle keepers.

As you look over the walls you can understand why this was such a strategically important place. Two significant dates in the founding of Bled and the castle are 1004 (a date you will often see around Bled) and 1011. In 1004 Emperor Henry ll of Germany gave his estate at Bled to Bishop Albuin of Brixen. Brixen today is in the Province of Bolzano in Italy's South Tyrol, a distance of over 260 kms, a 4-hour car journey in modern times. The second key date is 1011 when work began building the castle. First it was just the Romanesque tower which still stands behind high walls. Ironically, while over the centuries millions of people have come to visit Bled and the castle, the 11th and 12th century Bishops of Brixen did not.

This area was once the March (or Margraviate) of Carniola a south-eastern state of the Holy Roman Empire in the High Middle Ages, the predecessor of the Duchy of Carniola. The castle at that time were a possession of the Holy Roman Emperor. The Emperors' interests in the area – defensive, tax collection, development of the region – were carried out by the appointees and agents who lived and ruled from the castle.

This, the oldest castle in Slovenia is one of the country's principal tourist attractions, along with Postojna Cave, Lipica Stud Farm, and Ljubljana and its castle. Throughout the middle ages (and continuing up to the present day) additional buildings, towers and modifications were made to the castle. The building is organised around two court yards. At one time the castle servants would have lived in the outer area.

The gothic castle chapel on the upper courtyard was built in the 16th century and was renovated in the baroque style around 1700. The castle also houses a printing shop, wine cellar, forge, Knights' Hall, museum and café. The castle restaurant is said to be one of the best in Slovenia. You can drop in to eat during the day but call to reserve in the evening.

Because of the romantic setting, the castle – and really, all Bled – has become a favoured place for weddings. You never know, you might be inspired.

From the castle walls, you can post your photos directly to social media using the free wifi. Tag them #LakeBled or #Bledcastle and follow @Bledcastle on Twitter.

The castle website is [*www.blejski-grad.si/en*]

Bled Castle Events

The culture and entertainment of the middle ages are celebrated all summer long by the Knight Gašper Lambergar

Theatre Group. Dressed in costume, they demonstrate skills like medieval dances, knight duels, fire craft, and fire eating performances. The "Count and Countess of the castle" attend official visits, weddings and other events.

Exhibitions are held throughout the year in the upper gallery of the Printing Room. The paintings and photographs are usually by local and Slovenian artists.

Lectures and musical events are held throughout the year, and often the music events are for children and families.

Easter is celebrated with Easter egg hunts and games for children. There is a strong focus on events for children including some of the medieval themed events where children can become apprentice knights.

Medieval days – usually held during the first weekend in June. Medieval musicians 2 – 3 June

Other annual events include:

- Summer museum night.
- Baroque and medieval performances by the Cultural Society of Knight Gašper Lambergar held in the Upper Terrace from June to September, every Tuesday and Thursday, 5.00 pm.
- The castle plays host to some Festival Bled concerts in Knight's Hall and Okarina Festival in the Upper Terrace.
- As Halloween approaches the Medieval Camp sets up for a week in the parking area below the castle.
- The Halloween event for children is a specular afternoon and evening of games, dance, costume and face painting and a few scary, creepy things too.
- St. Martin's wine tasting. St Martin's Day is celebrated in Slovenia as the day that the grape juice turns to. There is traditional music and dancing, storytelling and a selection of wine and traditional food on the Upper Terrace.
- Christmas and New Year events are also held at the castle. For up to date information about events at Bled

Castle check their website [*www.blejski-grad.si/en*] and Bled Tourism website [*www.dled.si/en*]

Getting to and from Bled Castle

In the 11th and 12th century, castles were not built for easy access, quite the opposite they were built for protection. Consequently, in modern times castles are usually difficult to reach. Bled Castle is high above the town and the lake and if you are travelling by road the main entrance is at the top of Grajska cesta.

If you are driving from the town, take Prešernova cesta (traffic lights at the Pension Union/Union Bar) to where it meets Grajska cesta, the road to the carpark just outside the castle walls.

The travel agency Bled Tours organises daily trips to the castle. Departs: at 10.00 bus stop at Hotel Krim car park, and the main bus station in Bled, Returns: at 12:00 from the Castle car park. The cost is €20 per person (entrance ticket and return transfer included). Look out for the Bled Tours bus.

Contact details for Bled Tours: Jelovška cesta 25, 4260 Bled Mob: ++ 386 (0) 31 205 611 Tel: ++ 386 (0)4 574 35 20 www.bledtours.si and www.bled-taxi.com

Walking (I have even seen people jogging) from the town, there are some paths up the side of the hill. The easiest to access is from St. Martin's church.

The final path once you go over the draw bridge, is itself very steep. Inside there are lots of steps. The stunning views reward the effort, whether the day is bright and sunny or cloudy and moody. A photograph does not quite encapsulate the views across Gorenjska.

Bled Insider Knowledge:

Bled Castle is a well-known cultural monument which attracts crowds of visitors from all over the world. However, hidden in the forest of the Višče Hill under the

castle is a monument dedicated to Lord Adolf Muhr, a merchant from Vienna who owned Bled Castle between the years 1882 and 1919.

"Muhr built the villas Rog and Zlatorog on the shore of Lake Bled. Certainly, each are a dream location for everyone. Beside the monument, there is a bank where you can sit down and enjoy the view of the crystal-clear lake below, or just listen to the silence, or breathe in the fresh alpine air.

Lea Ferjan

PART 4 –
FOOD AND DRINK

The whole point of Firsthand Guides is to give you personal recommendations of places the writer has been. The suggestions are my personal choices. They are places I, my family and my friends like. I have not been to every pub, café and restaurant in Bled. I have been to most. I pay my own way and do not receive any inducements to write about these places. Here are my recommendations and further on the places on my wish list.

Best places for coffee (and 1 for tea)

My favourites and recommendations:

I cannot settle for one; I have these favourites, more or less in this order. They are each different, unique in their style. They do great coffee and snacks. The staff are helpful and friendly, and their menu extends beyond just coffee if you want to dally a little longer.

Caffe Peglez'n
cesta Svobode 8a, 4260 Bled, Slovenia

This is a very stylish little café, mentioned at the very beginning of the book as one of the first you find when you walk from the bus to the lake. Again, tiny inside but a large terrace where you get views of the lake and castle. The natural shade from overhanging trees protects you from the sun on the hottest days. There is room for children to play in this family friendly place. Caffe Peglez'n is favoured by locals as well as visitors. Good coffee, some snacks. A good place for an early start in the morning. It's usually open by 7:00 am when you can buy jam filled croissants (rogljički).

Art Café

cesta Svobode 7a, 4260 Bled, Slovenia
Phone: +386 4 576 71 79

It is popular with students from the business school and the hospitality college nearby and with younger tourists. People mostly sit outside. It is open from about 8:00 am. Simple snacks are available all day, and the coffee is very good.

The whole atmosphere changes when the evening approaches and Art Café turns into a party place. The bar stays open until the small hours, especially Friday and Saturday nights.

If you are in Bled in the winter, Art Café does great hot chocolate. Highly recommended.

Slaščičarna Zima

Grajska cesta 3, 4260 Bled, Slovenia
Phone: +386 4 574 16 16
www.smon.si

Slaščičarna Zima (until recently known as Slaščičarna Šmon) has been part of the culture of Bled for over 100 years. At the climax of Bled Nights when 15,000 candles float on the lake, they nestle in egg shells saved at there.

This cake shop fits into a category of its own, "best pastry on the planet", and would be very highly rated in any league of cafés and restaurants. The cakes are superb. The restaurant is famous, and it deserves the reputation. If you go nowhere else in Bled, walk up hill from the bus station and take coffee and cake here.

Apropos

Ljubljanska cesta 4, Bled 4260.
Phone: +386 4 574 40 44

There are six or seven places for coffee, drinks or food in the shopping centre. Music themed Apropos has the style and the tasteful background music as well as excellent coffee. It is a music themed tiny café with a larger seating area outside where the music theme continues.

Café Belvedere

Svobode 18, 4260 Bled, Slovenia
Phone: +386 (0)4 575 37 21
www.brdo.si/en/vila-bled/caf%C3%A9-belvedere

I think we can safely say that the pavilion has the best view of the island – you can almost reach out and touch the church. Known as "Tito's Tea Room", the historic building was designed by Jože Plečnik, the architect responsible for much of classic Ljubljana and parts of Kranj. It sits on stone stilts in the grounds of Vila Bled.

You can get to it via Hotel Bled or by the gate from the shore of the lake. If you are driving from Bled, past the main gates of Vila Bled following the road to the right and then you can drive to the small car park. Or you can walk that way, too.

Café Belvedere is open from 27 April to 8 June: 14.00 - 21.00. 9 June - 10 September: 10.00 - 21.00. 11 - 24 September: 10.00 - 19.00

Jasmin Tea Room

cesta Svobode 10, 4260 Bled, Slovenia
Phone: +386 4 574 38 27

If you are a tea drinker, after a few days in Slovenia you are going to be parched. Tea is a fruit infusion rather the dried leaf from India. Although Okarina Restaurant does a lovely marsala chai.

Hidden away from the hustle and bustle of a busy shopping area, Jasmin Tea Room is a small, interesting place beside the Tourist Information office. It rarely gets too busy and you can sit in the largish restaurant area or on the small terrace. It is one of the few places in Bled that serves excellent tea as well as fruit infusions. There is an accompanying shop a few metres away around the corner where you can buy tea, infusions, table-ware, cups, mugs, presents to bring home and tea-making paraphernalia.

K-Bar

Ljubljanska cesta 7, 4260 Bled, Slovenia
Phone: +386 31 382 055

Even though it is in the Hotel Krim building beside the EuropCar hire office and a hairdresser, K-Bar is a little off the beaten track. It is a cool and shaded place with good, value for money coffee and croissants (rogljički) in the morning.

Triglavska roža coffee shop at Infocenter Bled

Ljubljanska cesta 27, 4260 Bled

The Triglavska roža coffee shop is small, the choice is limited, but it is charming, and the setting is excellent. You can get breakfast in summer months there. The terrace there is very relaxed. Checkout the Infocenter's exhibitions and shop – but take some coffee and cakes.

Rowing Club Bled - Veslaški klub Bled

Župančičeva ulica 9, 4260 Bled, Slovenia
Phone: +386 40 220 886

This is the home of the Slovenian Olympic rowing team which has been garnering medals for more than 20 years. You can read all about their success and plans in the People In Bled section of this edition. The club hosts many competitions at European and World class levels each year and has been responsible for much of the development of Lake Bled's western shore.

The 20 to 25-minute walk (it's under 2 km, but you'll want to stop a few times) takes you to new ways of seeing the lake and the island – most of the photographs you see are from the south east and south shores.

The small café is complimented with a large terrace, a perfect place to sit in the late afternoon. You can also take the tourist train and make this your hop off point.

Shopping Centre Plaza

You can't miss it. Right under those multi-coloured canopies slap bang in the middle of the shopping centre. There is a group of separate seating areas distinguishable by the logos and colours. Which café serves you depends on where you sit. I have no particular recommendation, but out there in the open air, some nice views and a glass of Cockta and lots of ice. Cockta? Never heard of it? Read on ...

Insider Knowledge – Cockta

Looking for something non-alcoholic on a hot day to help cool you down? Yes, sure there is Pepsi and there is Coke, but why not drink something Slovenian? Cockta might look like one of those American imports, but it does not taste like them. The fizzy drink is made from some 11 herbs – the most prominent being rosehip. It was invented in the early 1950s in Slovenia (then part of Yugoslavia) when Coke and Pepsi were not available.

To quote one of its advertising slogans, "Brez kofeina - brez kisline - brez heca!" (No Caffeine - No Acid - No Joke!)

Best pubs

As in most of continental Europe, there is less of a pub culture than you find in the UK, the USA or Australia and New Zealand. More like France, bars here are usually restaurants and cafés as well. Some places change their character as the day progresses from coffee shop in the morning to loud party pub in the evening.

My favourites and recommendations:

With the usual caveat, these are my favourites and reflect my taste. There are two at the top of the list.

Pri Planincu

Grajska cesta 8, 4260 4260 Bled, Slovenia
Phone: +386 4 574 16 13

Small bar, part of a traditional restaurant with a pizzeria upstairs. This is the first bar I ever visited in Bled in 1996 and it is still the place I go to first. While the Belvedere Pavilion is historic for being the tea room of kings and presidents, Planincu is historic for being the pub of ordinary working people in Bled. Because, if you remove tourism from this town, it is essentially a rural farming community. Pri Planincu is part of the community, although, it attracts tourists in droves. The owner must be a motorbike fanatic. The walls and ceiling are decorated with vehicle number plates. I have spotted a motorbike in the rafters of the pizzeria. As mentioned earlier, many bars and restaurants in the region especially welcome bikers. This one positively encourages them.

The Kult Club

Ljubljanska cesta 4, 4260 Bled, Slovenia
www.facebook.com/KultBled/

In the shopping centre building but with a door onto the main road, this bar is for everyone one during the day but in the evening is much more for younger people. It is frequently used as a music venue. It is comfortable and plays a loud (but not too loud) music soundtrack during the day. On a hot day, it is cool and shaded inside.

I like the traditional bar features, the "at the movies" theme. There is an efficient service and a pretty good beer list, too.

I've not been there (and am unlikely to be there) in the evenings when the beat heats up. Keep an eye on the Facebook page for event announcements.

The George Best Back Bar

Grajska cesta 21a, 4260 Bled, Slovenia

This is an off the beaten track sports bar favoured by backpackers and adventure holiday makers during the summer. In the winter when the tourists are gone it is an after-work pub for locals. It is named after the Manchester United and Northern Ireland footballer George Best and consequently attracts supporters of both of those teams. It is a good basic bar and one of my regular haunts.

[New review] This is a hostel and sports bar, but regardless of when I visit the clientele is almost always Slovene, locals, people taking time away from work. Each year there seem to be fewer examples of George Best memorabilia. Last year the Holywood Northern Ireland Supporters Club framed poster had gone, this year the small George Best mural is painted over. There is a (commercially available) print marking George's funeral. As I leave I see a clock and pictures of London busses and Big Ben, something I cannot account for in this themed bar. The eclectic 1970s to 1990s rock sound track has been replaced by Slovenia's Radio 1. Change comes but losing the sports and in particular George Best and Manchester United theme to this bar would be a loss to Bled.

The beer is as it was, though and a good range - mainly lager. This is a pub with no pretentious. A plain bar for plain people. I love it, regardless. And soon it will be the nearest pub to the new car and coach park.

Bar Planinček

Prešernova cesta 11, 4260 Bled, Slovenia

This is a little bar and café hidden in plain sight between a bakery and the fire station (gasilski dom). It is small but perfectly formed. Although I have been inside, I more often have a beer outside, this is not a hot spot for tourism and that makes it a very welcoming and pleasant place to visit. Simple: beer (least expensive in town, possibly), coffee, snacks.

Pub Bled (Troha Pub)

cesta Svobode 19a, 4260 Bled, Slovenia
Phone: +386 4 574 26 22

Adjacent to the shopping centre this is a quiet and dark during the day often turning into a party pub in the evening. One of its advantages is that it is darker than most places in Bled, dark wood panels, dark wood tables, dark wood bar. The lights are low and not a lot of sunshine gets in. In other words, for many of us who have visited more than our fair share of bars, this is simply a pub. If you desire the sun, the light and the heat there is a small area outside where you can also smoke.

Devil Bar

cesta Svobode 15, 4260 4260 Bled, Slovenia

A large terrace outside and a large interesting interior. Once again, a place to escape on a hot afternoon. An enthusiastically loud party pub at night at the height of the summer. Inside it is beautiful; dark wood, high vaulted arched ceilings, tasteful décor. There is an extensive drinks menu, and attractively loud and active in the evenings.

Rock Bar

Ljubljanska cesta 5 Bled, Slovenia
Phone +386 41 622 526
Facebook https://en-gb.facebook.com/ROCKROCKROCKbarbled/

The "Bikers Welcome" sign is at the door. Opening at 6:00 am, Rock Bar can be quiet during the day, although when town is busy, it is busy, too. Evening and night time is when this place comes to life. As you would expect the crowd is young(er) but not exclusively young and music is an important attraction. It is at the edge of the parking area and near the Sports Hall Bled (Športna dvorana Bled) complex.

Tiger Bar (Stari Tiger)

Cesta svobode 2, Bled, Slovenia
Phone +386 31 674 901

Facebook www.facebook.com/Tiger-bar-403727413047872/

Almost opposite the bus station this is a cheap, cheerful bar with good fast service, a range of authentic Slovenian and central European food. Most of the seating and service is outside under shady chestnut trees.

It is among the earliest opening bars and restaurants in Bled with morning coffee served from 6:00 am and closes at midnight.

If you are going to eat there (and are a meat eater) focus on the local specialities like ćevapčići – skinless meat sausage. It tastes better than that description.

Dnevni Bar Škrbina

Cesta svobode 1, Bled, 4260 Bled

Flags of world may flutter around the terrace of this classic Bled bar, but it is not a sophisticated tourist pub. But it is friendly and welcoming. It is close to the bus. 0.5l of Union is €2.40 a bela kava €1.80 about what you would expect to pay. It's a bar for locals. It is a perfectly decent place. If you are fed up with fellow tourists and want a quiet break from them, this is worth considering.

Krčma Bar

Cesta svobode 8a, Bled 4260, Slovenia
Phone +386 70 732 799

Krčma Bar is in the square with Hotel Jelovica on one side, the cycle hire and the phone shops on the other, looking out at the hotel coach park and beyond that the bus station and Pri Planincu. The terrace is comfortable and roomy. Inside more intimate. The welcome warm and genuine. But it is comparatively expensive. A half-litre bottle of Lašco at €2.80 (€2.20 in George Best) one wonders why? If you prefer coffee, €2.30 for a Bela Kava (flat white) which is €1.80 around the corner. Perhaps it's better value for money in the evening when a younger party loving crowd can be found there. (Prices May 2018)

Best pizza

Pizza is very popular in Slovenia, and not just among tourists. The pizzerias (sometimes spelt the Slovenian way, picerija) I have been to in Bled and Ljubljana are of a very high standard, I've never had a disappointing pizza, so this list might be a little redundant. However, there is more to a pizza than a base and topping. The place where you eat and the service that you get can make all the difference. These 5 suggestions are not the only places to get pizza in Bled, but they are places "hand on heart" that I can recommend. Each have extensive menus with dozens of toppings to choose from. You will always be able to buy excellent pizza in Bled for between €8 and €10.

Pri Planincu Pizza

Grajska cesta 8, 4260 4260 Bled, Slovenia
Phone: +386 4 574 16 13
www.pri-planincu.com

You might have already noted I have nominated Pri Planincu as my favourite bar. It's also on the list for favourite restaurants for Slovenian food. It happens to be one of my favourite places overall. Even travel writers have favourite places. The restaurant is upstairs, traditionally Alpine with wood panelling and wooden decorations. There are dozens of toppings, beer at a reasonable price and great service. There is a small terrace open in the good weather. This is a family friendly place where English, German and Italian are spoken or understood.

Pizzeria Gallus

Ljubljanska cesta 4, Bled 4260, Slovenia
Phone: +386 4 574 32 99
www.pizzeriagallus.si/

This is as good a pizzeria as anywhere. From the terrace on the second floor of the shopping centre you can look out at the activity below. Inside it is cool and comfortable. The prices compare well with all the other pizzerias in Bled, the variety of toppings excellent and the base size, generous.

Picerija Briksen

Ljubljanska cesta 5, 4260 Bled, Slovenia
Phone: +386 40 652 995
www.pizzerijabriksen.com

You will find Briksen at the Sports Hall. I have only ever been inside to order and to pay; almost everyone eats outside under the shade of the big umbrellas. It is a sunny spot almost all day. You will find a good selection of toppings. Look out for a special celebration pizza for the Slovenia hockey team's performance at Sochi winter Olympics. In addition to pizza there are burgers, sandwiches.

Pizzeria Rustika

Riklijeva cesta 13, 4260 Bled, Slovenia
Phone: +386 4 576 89 00
www.pizzeria-rustika.si

Rustika has a very good reputation and is often said to make the best pizza in Bled. I don't agree, I'm not sure there is a "best". Here the cooking is very good, the pizzas first class. You will not be disappointed. The restaurant is a little away from the town centre, up the hill towards St. Martin's church. It is particularly cosy in the colder days of autumn and winter. It has a delivery service.

Recommended restaurants

You will find most if not all the restaurants in Bled offer local dishes. Sometimes there will be modern twists on traditional cooking. A few specialise in traditional – some might say "hearty" – dishes which satisfy the most voracious appetite. The area is rich in fresh easily sourced ingredients. It's a safe guess that noting you eat will have travelled very far.

At the end of this chapter there are examples of some of local specialities.

Let's start with my top 10 restaurants

Public & Vegan Kitchen Bled

Ljubljanska cesta 4, 4260 Bled, Slovenia
Phone: +386 70 270 712

In a shaded, slightly secluded corner of the main shopping centre, you will find Bled's only vegan restaurant. In 2014 a very small vegan place called Zaziv opened offering vegan burgers. Public Kitchen opened before Zaziv moved to Ljubljana full time.

While you will find food suitable for vegetarians in almost every restaurant in Bled, Open Kitchen is the only place dedicated specifically to vegans. The main offering is vegan burgers. Choose one of four patties, then one of four breads, then the sauce.

Forget what you know about fast food burger joints. The chef will not begin to build your burger until you order. I use the word "build" advisedly. In the basket delivered to your table, a burger as high as it is wide. A diameter of about six inches and a height of at least four inches. The salad is crunchy fresh, the patty warm when it arrives. Ask for knife and fork ... and extra napkins. You are about to do battle.

I am a meat eater, but meat or no meat this is a first-class burger. You do not need to be a vegan to appreciate it.

Beside me an elderly American couple are finishing their salad and arranging to collect a picnic tomorrow morning, and perhaps bring more of their favourite salads with them to eat on the flight home at the weekend.

Good food, well priced. Closed Mondays Opens 12:00 noon to 9:00 pm

Pri Planincu

Grajska cesta 8, 4260 4260 Bled, Slovenia
Phone: +386 4 574 16 13
www.pri-planincu.com

Yes, this is the same Pri Planincu featured in Best Bar and Best Pizza, and no they are not paying for favourable reviews nor feeding me for free. It just happens this is my favourite place. The restaurant is old and a bit faded – that's why I like it. The food is traditional Slovenian homemade fare and is consistently good (I've been eating there for over 20 years.) If your grandmother was from Carniola, this is what her home would be like ... possibly. It is excellent for budget travellers, but you find plenty of people arriving in expensive cars eating there too. It is also a favourite of locals.

Finefood - Penzion Berc

Želeška cesta 15, 4260 Bled, Slovenia
Phone: +386 4 574 18 38
www.penzion-berc.si/si

The Berc family run the Hotel Garni Berc (Luka's property) and Pension Berc (Miha's place). Both, rightly, score outstanding reviews for their accommodation and hospitality. Pension Berc has one of the best restaurants in Bled. It is a special place, a restaurant to treat yourself.

It is relaxed and semi-formal, that is to say the waiting staff professional and formal, and guests are more relaxed informal. We are sitting in a group of four tables and before long, the young couple from the Netherlands, the Canadian couple and the retirees from California are swapping stories with us about what they have done today, where they have come from, what their plans are.

The food is outstanding. You have a choice between the €46, 4 course tasting menu and the a la carte. Specialities include fish (on our visit sea bass, bream and trout), Istrian pastas, Angus beef, game medallions, light soups. All beautifully cooked and presented.

The Slovene wine list includes white, red, orange and fizz. The waiter will give you advice if you need it.

One final thought: pumpkin oil. If you have not tried it, do.

Outstanding. Dober tek

More here www.laliste.com/en/laliste/worldOštarija Babji zob
cesta Svobode 8, 4260 Bled, Slovenia
Phone: +386 8381-0584
www.ostarija-babjizob.si/en

Two years elapsed between my first and second visit to this restaurant. It was good the first time and even better the second.

The restaurant is named after the great rock by the Jelovice plateau "Babji zob" or "Old hag's tooth". It has narrowed its menu of simple food, with lots of Balkan grill and very large portions, to something more sophisticated, better quality, better service, better atmosphere. Ostarija-Restaurant Babji Zob has shifted up a gear while keeping excellent value for money.

In the summer time the terrace is busy and in the winter the bar-restaurant is warm, cosy and welcoming. The reduced menu focuses more on the quality of cooking and presentation. There are several small "rooms" inside where people site close together and the result is a marvellous atmosphere.

On a cold winter's evening it is a welcoming and warm place to visit for a beer or a bowl on mushroom soup.

Restaurant Sova Bled

cesta Svobode 37, 4260 Bled, Slovenia
Reservations: +386 59 132 100
www.restavracija-sova.com

The Sova restaurant is about to enter its third year in its present location in Mlino on the southern shore of Lake Bled, a 25-minute walk from the town centre. Sova is in an old bar and before becoming a very good restaurant was a pizzeria with a good Slovenian home-made style of cooking.

The standard of cuisine has been elevated and while the restaurant still looks like pretty standard bar, the food is outstanding. Modern Slovenian cooking takes place behind the bar in a small kitchen. The staff are very helpful especially choosing the right wines and guiding you through the occasionally slightly obscure menu.

It is a mid-range price but very good cooking and an interesting menu. I often choose the Sova Krožnik. It is similar to a Balkan grill, but more sophisticated.

Pension Mlino

cesta Svobode 45, 4260 Bled, Slovenia
Phone: +386 4 574 14 04
www.mlino.si

Pension Mlino is a beautiful building and busy restaurant, bar and B&B. Here you find traditional Slovenian hospitality, excellent traditional Slovenian food and the day's soundtrack is traditional Gorenjska music playing in the background.

There is more than one restaurant in the building, but the bar is the place to drop in for a drink or food. You will find it directly opposite the pletna pier in Mlino. This is where the pletnar, who row passengers to the island, gather after their shift.

This is another personal favourite for lunch, dinner or just a bowl of mushroom soup on a cold day. In summer, it can become very busy as the tour bus passengers disembark at that point.

If you are a couple and like fish, the fish feast is one of the best items on the menu.

Gostilna Murka

Riklijeva cesta 9, 4260 Bled, Slovenia
Phone: +386 4 574 33
www.gostilna-murka.com

If you like traditional, there are fewer more traditional places than this. It was established in 1906 in the old part of town. The restaurant is light, with plenty of room. The service is pitch perfect. It has a good reputation for traditional cooking and entertainment. A simple Slovenian dinner will be inexpensive. The restaurant is "in the round" and is bright and airy on a warm evening.

Oštarija Peglez'n

cesta Svobode 19, 4260 Bled, Slovenia
Phone: +386 4 574 42 18
bit.ly/2BrxyCQ [Facebook]

Oštarija Peglez'n, close to the shopping centre and opposite the Restavracija Panorama, will always be on the short list of best places to eat in Bled, unless something drastic happens. And in the years that I have been going, it has only got better. One evening, walking past I noticed a queue to get in. A rare event in Bled.

In the summer on the small terrace the sunlight streams in as it begins its descent behind the Julian Alps. Large blinds are lowered and even though you are just a few steps from a main road, you feel removed from the busy street. Inside the main restaurant the décor is traditional Slovenian home kitchen.

Before we visited, people had recommended Oštarija Peglez'n for the fish. Yes, sure, but the menu is all good and reliable. The service is great. If you are new to Slovenia and want to try some Slovenian wine with dinner, this the place to ask advice.

Always a favourite.

Restavracija Okarina

Ljubljanska cesta 8, 4260 Bled, Slovenia
Phone: +386 4 574 14 58
www.okarina.com/en/
Opening hours: Seasonal – 12 noon –11 pm not open year-round.

Another favourite with visitors and locals. There has been an Okarina restaurant in Bled for more than 30 years, starting in a different building to the one now established on the busy road in the centre of town. The restaurant shares its name with and is responsible for the world/ethno music festival held annually in Bled.

Brightly decorated with superb paintings, good service and a style unique in Bled.

You should expect, in addition to the usual, good vegetarian food and spicy Indian food. Leo the owner is a vegetarian who visits India every year. Paul McCartney ate there, he liked it.

Peking Chinese Restaurant

Ulica narodnih herojev 3, 4260 Bled, Slovenia
Phone: +386 4 574 17 16

I have walked past this restaurant so many times and each time thought about dropping in. It's large terrace almost always has customers at tables all through the day and always in the evening. My focus in Slovenia has been to find Slovenian food. I love Chinese food but going there seemed to be a slight distraction. I resisted one evening recently and I am mighty glad I did.

I went for the terribly predictable sweet and sour chicken. At least I had something to compare it with. The taste was different to what I am used to. St home the "sour" tends towards citric, here it was different, a deeper taste. The fried rice had macedoine of peas and carrots mixed in (and was priced separately) the chicken dumplings were generous in size and quantity. It was on the expensive side. Had I ordered the steamed rice the difference in cost would have been noticeable.

Excellent.

Next, 6 of the best of the rest

Vila Prešeren

Veslaška promenada 14, 4260 Bled, Slovenia
Phone: +386 4 575 25 10
www.villa-preseren.com/

On a sunny day the open-air terrace is busy with tourists and locals sitting beside one of the best spots on the lake shore. No more than a patch of grass and a pathway separates Vila Prešeren from the lake. In the summer evenings, musicians play. Drop by for coffee after shopping or a beer after a walk around the lake which can turn into a full-scale lunch or even dinner. Coffee, cakes and drinks are good. Lunch – often specialities from Bled and Slovenia – is one of the best in the town. Although I've never been to dinner, the menu would suggest this is not a place for people on a tight budget. During the summer Taste Bled festival, Vila Prešeren is probably one of the best places to go to try traditional Bled and Slovenian cooking.

Restavracija Vila Ajda Dax

cesta Svobode 27, 4260 Bled, Slovenia
Phone: +386 4 576 83 20
www.vila-ajda.si/

Vila Ajda is one of the grand houses built in the 18th and early 19th century that are dotted around Lake Bled. It is now one of the best restaurants in Bled used by visitors and locals alike. For the last seven years, it has been run by Vlado Dakskobler, "Everybody calls me Dax."

The food is strongly Slovenian and Carniolan. The menu ranges from the humble struklji (one of the most characteristic everyday Slovenian dishes, usually made from cottage cheese rolled-up in dough) and Balkan meats like čevapčići (grilled minced beef), and ražnjići (skewered meats) through to chateaubriand. But Dax points out jelenov medaljon (deer medallions) as one of the highlights for him.

And the menu – which changes four times a year to reflect the season – uses ingredients and dishes from the wider geographical area with Italian and Austrian taking their place. Some dishes are from very specific areas such as Mojstrana and Dvoje, villages in the Alps between Bled and Kranjska Gora.

If it is on the menu, try a house special; pečene ripsi reba brez maščobe (literally ribs and veal shank baked without fat). It is served with roast vegetables – with a slight bite – in a pan which is at lunchtime probably enough for two people. Slovenian portions are often extremely generous.

The house wine here is Erzetic, a family owned winery in Goriška Brda.

Vrtnarija - Garden Village

cesta Gorenjskega odreda 16, 4260 Bled.
Phone: +386 (0) 838 99 221
www.gardenvillagebled.com/

In June 2018, Garden Village became the first Glamping site in the world to be awarded 6 stars by World of Glamping. The 'Greenhouse' restaurant at Garden Village boasts "Slovenian Cuisine Vrtnarija – fresh from our garden to your plate."

Vrtnarija is among the most interesting and innovative restaurants in Bled. Situated in Mlino about 200m from the lake, it creates its own style bringing the outside, inside. The Garden Village "glamping" site opened in 2014 and the restaurant is part of this new development.

Yes, that is real grass growing (and carefully tended) on the tables – bringing a whole new meaning to "Surf and Turf" (as if they served anything so ordinary). And that is little stream running through the restaurant and a tiny foot bridge to cross it. The first time we ate there was just a simple lunch – sandwich and a glass of wine by the pool. It was terrific.

The second time we visited was with a couple of local VIPs and we had the Chef's Tasting Menu. It was delicious. The food is unmistakably Slovenian – but modern and looks as good as it tastes, and the bill matches the high standard.

Restavracija Grill

Best Western Premier Hotel Lovec
Ljubljanska 6 4260 Bled, Slovenia
Phone: +386 (0) 4 620 41 26
www.grill-bled.com/

The Grill serves some very good food. It is unlikely that you will be disappointed. We have only been there twice. The service was efficient.

Hint: better in than out. With the town's shopping centre and car park to one side and the busy main road to another, this is not the quietest or most romantic spot in Bled. Inside is a lot more comfortable.

The BBQ burgers, while not prominent on the menu, have some lovely regional twists. The burgers are usually one of the features of the Taste of Bled exhibition held during the summer. The meat for the patties, the chef told me, is sourced from a nearby farm.

There is a strong traditional Slovenian theme to their menu. Each Thursday, from 15 June to 21 September at 7:00 pm they hold a Slovenian speciality event. Their example menu prices are mid-range.

Vila Bled

cesta Svobode 26, 4260 Bled, Slovenia
Phone +386 (0) 4 575 37 10
www.brdo.si/en/vila-bled/vila-bled

Vila Bled has had an interesting history. Before the building that sits on the land now, there was a grand castle. It was pulled down – reports from the time said the men working on the site had tears in their eyes as they destroyed the building. Vila Bled was built after WWII and was summer home of President Tito. After Slovenia's independence, it became a hotel - part of a French chain - and is now owned by the Slovenian government.

The hotel gets all the reviews - and generally very high scores. The restaurant tends to be overlooked by reviewers. Yes, it is expensive, one of a clutch of restaurants in Bled that might put a dent in your credit card. Overall, Slovenia is not an expensive place to dine and, in that context, Vila Bled is expensive. Yet compared with a similar standard restaurant in most European capitals, it is very good value.

If you are on a budget but want the experience, try lunch on the terrace on a sunny afternoon. The views are stunning - island, church, castle, pletna, St Martin's, and the edge of town. We love it. Even if you are not planning to use the restaurant, Vila Bled should be on your list of places to see. The extensive grounds are open to the public and are very pleasant for an amble. Parts, beyond the Belvedere Café are now abandoned and overgrown, including what I am told was once a private zoo.

Inside the hotel there is a small display of photos of world leaders who stayed there during Tito's time along with Tito's desk. Today some world leaders still stay at the hotel; Bled is often the venue for major regional political events including Bled Strategic Forum.

Park Restaurant and Café

cesta Svobode 15, 4260 Bled, Slovenia
Phone: +386 4 579 18 18
bit.ly/2BpUjXP [Sava Hotels website]

This is the home of the legendary Bled Cream Cake which is celebrated here when the town's summer season officially begins. Yes, a cream cake party. Often in the evening during the summer, there is live music.

The terrace views are great; the castle, the lake and the island. The seating is comfortable and the atmosphere outside is very pleasant. You are seated and served quickly. The staff are usually friendly, and efficient. However, in recent years, they have become stretched and while your order arrives quickly it can take time attracting attention to get your bill before you leave. If you are not staying long, ask for your bill with your order.

When it is busy I prefer to sit inside the restaurant. The coffee is good, the lunchtime sandwiches are good and reasonably priced. You still have the views from behind the glass. On a hot day, it is a good place to escape to.

During the winter season, the terrace becomes an ice rink where families gather to skate and take hot chocolate (vroča čokolada) and mulled wine (kuhano vino).

Finally, still on my Wish List

This is not "the best of the rest", because I know that many below are outstanding and could top any list. But, I have not been to any of them and can't give a firsthand account.

Penzion Mayer

Želeška cesta 7, 4260 Bled, Slovenia
Phone: +386 4 576 57 40
www.mayer-sp.si/

Close to Hotel Garni Berc (which is consistently voted best place to stay in Bled – I've stayed; it is). Like its neighbour Pension Berc, it has an outstanding reputation and is in a beautiful setting away from all the crowds and the lake and near the Rikli Balance (formerly Golf) Hotel. Without having tried, I can still recommend that you do, simply based on their reputation.

Restaurant 1906

Hotel Triglav, Kolodvorska 33, 4260 Bled, Slovenia
Phone: +386 (0)4 575 26 10
www.hoteltriglavbled.si/en/restavracija-1906-bled

High above Bled overlooking almost the whole lake from Triglav Hotel. Modern Slovenian cooking and Slovenian wines. It has an outstanding reputation. I did one have a very good lunch there and, on that basis, would recommend it. The hotel and restaurant are both used by Bled and Slovenian rowing teams for VIP visitors, so that must be a recommendation itself.

Topolino Restaurant

Ljubljanska cesta 26, Bled 4260, Slovenia

Phone: +386 4 574 17 81

It is really not far out of town; mere few minutes' walk. Yet it remains on my wish list. You always have to have something to look forward to.

Bled Castle Restaurant

Grajska cesta 61, 4260 Bled, Slovenia
Phone: +386 4 620 34 4
bit.ly/2CR02lG [restaurant website]

The Caste Restaurant has the reputation of being one of the top restaurants in all of Slovenia. There is no question that it has the best view.

Astoria Hotel Restaurant
Address: Prešernova cesta 44, 4260 Bled, Slovenia
Phone: +386 4 579 44 00

There are plenty of hotel restaurants, but this one is special as it is recommended by sports people and it is the training restaurant for the Bled hotel and catering college.

Restavracija Arbor

Ljubljanska cesta 4, 4260 Bled, Slovenia
Phone: +386 4 574 30 33
www.arborbled.si/about-arbor

In the shopping centre this looks like a very attractive simple restaurant with a big choice of Slovenian and Mediterranean food on a well-priced menu. I notice they do pizza. It is on my list of places to test.

Restavracija Julijana

Toplice Hotel cesta Svobode 12, 4260 Bled, Slovenia
Phone: +386 4 579 10 00
bit.ly/2BRlhHf [restaurant website]

I have not had dinner or lunch here, but if you are feeling flush, they do a splendid breakfast before 9.30 am

The Toplice is at the high-end of the high-end. It is luxuriously decorated, how I imagine a Viennese drawing room might be decorated. You can go into look around the public rooms or take coffee. If you do, check out the display cabinet with photos of many political and entertainment celebrities, royalty, and other notables.

Insider Knowledge

Donald and Melania Trump at Toplice Hotel Restaurant

Sitting in Penzion Mlino after a particularly good dinner, we were chatting with our young waiter. We had got to know many of the staff well during our stay on the south shore of Lake Bled. "You know," said the waiter pointing at one of his colleagues. "He was once President Trump's butler." The older man, who served dishes with the grace of an orchestral conductor, sensed he was the subject of the conversation. He joined the conversation.

As most people know by now, the US First Lady, Melania Trump is from Slovenia. What might be less well known is that she is no stranger to Bled. It is understood that this is where she began her modelling career. The local story has it that there was once a garment factory just outside the town – around where the new Mercator has been built. The owners occasionally hired her to model their products. Two years before she married Donald Trump, the couple made a quick trip to Slovenia to meet Melania's parents.

The then Mr. Trump and Melania landed at the airport and were swiftly transported to the Toplice Grand Hotel in the

centre of Bled, overlooking the lake. It is a place where royalty – including Prince Charles – has stayed and where politicians and leading business people stay during the Bled Strategic Forum.

"Yes." A friend whose family goes back for generations in Bled told me, "I saw them on the terrace."

The waiter in the Penzion Mlino who had joined us was working in the Toplice at the time. He had been appointed the visiting party's personal butler for the visit. He pulls out his phone to proudly show me a photograph of the Trump party and himself.

Within three hours of landing, he tells me, they were back at Brnik airport and departing Slovenia.

Beyond Bled
Gostilna Zatrnik Pr' Jagru

Zatrnik-Hrnica 82, 4247 Zg. Gorje
Phone: +386 599 60272
www.gostilna-zatrnik.si/

This is really something different. If you are a hiker, you might just come across this fascinating place on your walks. You could drive by on your way to or from Pokljuka. On the road, almost in the middle of nowhere (it is in fact near quite a lot of places, but somehow seems remote) this restaurant is famous for its hog roast. Suckling pig on a spit, very large helpings. Not a place to bring a vegetarian. Superb, rustic, authentic. Check the website for directions and menus [*www.gostilna-zatrnik.si/*].

"Too much info. Decide for me, Davy!"

It is obvious, but there is too much to choose from. If we met on the bus to Bled from Ljubljana and wanted my immediate suggestions, I would ask a few questions first, such as where you are staying. In Mlino I have no hesitation recommending Sova and Pension Mlino, for example. If you really want to treat yourself, Vila Bled.

But let's suppose you are going to be around Bled centre and only have a couple of days to visit. Here are my personal suggestions for 2018.

Quick coffee: Both Caffe Peglez'n and Art Café.

Restaurants: Either Oštarija Babji zob or Oštarija Peglez'n.

Pizza: Pri Planincu or Gallus

Pub: This is more difficult. What's really missing in Bled is a specialist beer and craft beer pub. Kult and Pri Planincu are my suggestions. Kult especially in the evening.

Top end restaurant: If you want to spoil yourself or someone else, I suggest Bled Castle restaurant or Pension Berc.

Specialist: Public Kitchen and Okarina for vegetarians and vegans.

The Best in Slovenia
In December 2017, French Publication La Liste published the best restaurants in Slovenia. Around 1000 of the top restaurants from around the world are listed each year. The 2017/2018 list includes 5 restaurants from Slovenia.

The best Slovenian restaurant in their estimation is the **Gostinstvo Mak** in Maribor under the direction of chef David Vračko.
Osojnikova ulica 20, 2000 Maribor, Slovenia. Phone: +386 2 620 00 53 www.restavracija-mak.si/

The list included

Cubo in Ljubljana
Šmartinska cesta 55, 1000 Ljubljana, Slovenia. Phone: +386 1 521 15 15, www.cubo-ljubljana.com/en

Dam in Nova Gorica,
Ulica Vinka Vodopivca 24, 5000 Nova Gorica, Slovenia. Phone: +386 5 333 11 47, www.restavracija-dam.si

JB Restaurant (chef Janez Bratovž) Ljubljana
Miklošičeva 19 SI-1000 Ljubljana, Phone: +386 1 430 70 70
info@jb-slo.com, jb-slo.com/en/

Hiša Franko led by one of Slovenia's greatest chefs Ana Roš,
Staro selo 1, 5222 Kobarid, Slovenia, Phone: +386 5 389
4120, info@hisafranko.com, www.hisafranko.com/en

More here *www.laliste.com/en/laliste/world*

Some favourite Slovenian dishes

If you are a "foodie" and want to experience the best of the
whole area, the Slovenian Alps Taste Gorenjska brochure can
be downloaded here [bit.ly/2DlQjVu]. It will tell you about
the specialities from each of the town in the regions.

This is a very small selection of items you might see on a
menu. If you are a bit more hesitant about trying new tastes,
give these a go as an introduction.

Mushroom soup

I don't know what it is, the freshness of the mushrooms
picked within a mile or two from the kitchen where the soup
is made or if there is some special ingredient? The mushroom
soup here – in every restaurant I have tried it, it marvellous.
Often a meal in itself.

If you know what you are doing, there is mushroom picking
in the forests around Pokljuka. Any restaurant in Bled serves
good mushroom soup. If you want something different,
though, take a short journey to Radovljica and in the old
town there are two excellent restaurants. The more
traditional of the two is Gostilna Lectar which serves the
soup in a loaf of bread.

Štruklji

With chives or with walnuts or goodness knows how many
other variations. It has been a part of Slovenian cuisine for
over 500 years. In its simplest form štrukelji is rolled and
filled dumplings. In these parts, the dough is rolled and filled

with cottage cheese. I have had it with a light sprinkling of sugar, too.

Almost any restaurant will serve it as an alternative to potato, for example. A good traditional place to try it is Pension Mlino.

Kranjska klobasa (Carniolan sausage)

This is a big favourite here – and all around this region and beyond. This is a large pork sausage, often served as a pair. Kranjska klobasa is a protected name under European law and only one from this region can have that name. Be careful as you cut into one, they have been known to spit back.

Try them in Gostilna Murka.

Ričet

Ričet is a traditional dish found in Slovenian and beyond in Croatia, Austria and Bavaria. It is a thick soup. In other parts of this book you will read about St Martin's Day when the grape juice turns to wine and the outdoor festivals to celebrate. Ričet is often available to warm the hungry party goer. The main ingredients are pot barley, beans, potatoes, carrots, parsley, celery, leeks, tomatoes, onions, and garlic. And there should be a good portion of cured pork in it.

The Slovenian Alps Taste Gorenjska brochure recommends Gostišče klub Kovač in Naklo for ričet. Naklo is about 20km south-east of Bled. They tell me that it is on the menu but not all year round. There is a good bus service from Bled, it is on the route to and from Ljubljlana. If you want to explore food, it could be worth your time stopping off for an hour or two.

Potica

This is a celebration cake traditionally prepared for Christmas day and is something of an annual test for whomever is cooking at home. As with any traditional food, family recipes are handed down from one generation to the next. After the kneaded dough is left to rise, it is rolled-out covered in the filling and tightly rolled up before cooking.

It contains honey, vanilla essence, ground cinnamon, ground cloves, lemon peel, and rum.

Fortunately, you neither have to wait for Christmas nor an invitation to someone's home. Potica is standard fare and while there are variations, you should look for hazelnut potica with figs from Bled Island.

Bled Cream Cake

Available everywhere in Slovenia. The Park Restaurant is the home to Bled cream cake. My favourite is Slaščičarna Zima.

Slovenian Wine

New for 2018:

There are plans to hold the 1st Bled Wine Festival over three days in August. At time of writing there is limited information, but I understand that more than 20 Slovenian winemakers will exhibit along the lakeshore promenade from 10th to 12th August. Expect Slovenian food and music, for what is wine without either?

St Martin's Day

Let's begin with a celebration. The annual celebration of Slovenian wine is held throughout the country on 11 November – St Martin's day. St. Martin is the patron saint of wine makers and on that day (and for a few days before and several days afterwards, the best new Slovenian wine is celebrated around the country. Traditionally it is the day that the grape must turns to wine. In some restaurants before that date you can buy a glass of must (try Pension Mlino).

Throughout the country the day will be marked by events called Pot Sv. Martina (St Martin's way or St Martin's route). Wine growers set up stalls, glasses can be hired and for a reduced price you can sample as many wines as you like Each event is organised in a slightly different way. You usually hire out a wine glass, sometimes you pay a set price, sometimes you buy tickets. Simple food is cooked on site. Often there is music and entertainment. The atmosphere is always happy and friendly.

In 2018, St. Martin's day will be celebrated above the lake in Bled Castle, beside the lake in Spa Park. There will be events in Kranj and in Ljubljana, too. And, further afield especially in the wine growing regions. Stalls will have samples of wine and Slovenian food.

Because of the weather, of all the times to visit Bled, Gorenjska, Ljubljana, early November is not the most appealing. The vast bulk of tourists have gone, the sky is often cloudy. The weather can be stormy.

Spa Park Bled

What happens? The 2018 St Martin's Day celebrations will (weather permitting) be held in Spa Park on 11 November. Wine growers will set up stalls and offer tastings. If you like what you taste and want to buy, there is a big selection to choose from.

Then there is the food – simple, warming, and traditional made there and then. It's like a friendly polite drinks party, but everyone's well wrapped up against the elements.

Bled Castle

You can choose wine from the cellar in Bled Castle all year round. And they don't always mess around with corkscrews. Sometimes a sword does a better job – the bottle's neck is swiftly and efficiently sliced off. The St Martin's Day celebration is on the upper terrace, more wine, more food, music and entertainment including traditional dances. Get there early.

Kranj

Unless there is a special event, or you are with a guided tour, you can't get access to the city's famous ancient catacombs. That is where Pot Sv. Martina is held. As the event can attract more than 3,000 people each year, you must book in advance with Kranj Tourism.

More information:

Kranj Tourism
www.visitkranj.com/en/events/top-events/wine-route
Zavod za turizem in kulturo Kranj
Glavni trg 2, 4000 Kranj
Phone+386 (0)4 238 04 50
E-mail: info@visitkranj.si

Ljubljana

Another open-air event which can fall foul of the vagaries of the weather, the Ljubljana Wine Route is held over and around the Triple Bridge and along Stritarjeva ulica up to the City Hall.

Scores of stalls from all over the country with wine, hot food and all sorts of other tempting buy-ables are available.

All these celebrations are held around 11 November – sometimes the weekend before or after. As they are outdoor events, they will be subject to weather. Check with the organisers before going.

More Information

Tourism Ljubljana
www.visitljubljana.com/
Address and general information

Krekov trg 10, 1000 Ljubljana

Phone +386 (0)1 306 45 83
e-mail: info@visitljubljana.si

Tourist information centre

Ljubljana Tourist Information Centre – TIC
Adamič-Lundrovo nabrežje 2, 1000 Ljubljana
Phone: +386 (0)1 306 12 15
e-mail: tic@visitljubljana.si

Maribor

Slovenia's second city, Maribor, is the centre of some of the biggest celebrations of St. Martin's Day. This is the home of the oldest vine in the world. At more than 400 years old, the Old Vine is a symbol of the rich wine culture of Maribor, Styria, and all of Slovenia. There is a cutting of the vine growing in Bled Castle.

On St. Martin's Day there is a "ceremonial christening of must" to mark the change into wine, the arrival of the wine queen. Trg Leona Štuklja in the city centre, is the place to find wine tastings, food, music and entertainment.

Maribor is also a perfect starting point to follow the Wine Roads here any time of the year. Look especially at the Jeruzalem Wine Route.

For more about the oldest vine in the world

> The Old Vine House
> Vojašniška 8, 2000 Maribor
> *www.staratrta.si*
>
> Open October to April, 9:00 am to 6:00 pm May to September until 8:00 pm

Phone: +386 (0)2 25 15 100 +386 (0)51 335 521
e-mail: stara-trta@maribor.si

Find out more about the Wine Roads and Wine Routes *www.slovenia.si/visit/cuisine/wines/wine-routes/*

Wine by numbers:

> 3 wine-growing regions, 14 wine-growing districts, 52 vine varieties, 22,300 hectares of vineyards, 28,000 wineries, 80 million litres of wine annually

Wine Growing Regions

My first introduction to Slovenian wine was in 1997 during a visit to Jeruzalem area near the Hungarian and Croatian borders. From a town called Ormož, I visited Jeruzalem and Ljutomer, tasted ice wine in a celler somewhere deep in the countryside, and ate Slovenian beef goulash (goveji golaž), with buckwheat if I remember correctly. It is difficult to find, but not impossible, Slovenian wine outside the country. Three-quarters of the wine produced in these vinyards stays in Slovenia which means – if you like wine – when you visit, you must try some.

10 years ago – March 2008 – British wine writer Jancis Robinson was one of the first people to bring Slovenian viniculture to the general consumer in an article for the Financial Times. Most of the wineries she visited were at the western side of the country bordering Italy on the dramatic slopes of Brda. If you are a wine aficionado, you might find what Jancis Robinson recorded useful. 150 notes can be found here: bit.ly/2BY4ORq [Jancis Robinson's website]

Podravska

Here, bordering Croatia and Hungary in the east, is where I began my exploration of Slovenian wine. Podravje is Slovenia's largest wine region. Here you will find lots of varieties of white wine (barely any red is produced) along with sparking and dessert wines. Here you will find Prekmurje and Štajerska wineries.

Posavska

We've moved south from Podravska, but not far. This time on the border of Croatia, you will find the Bizeljsko Sremič, Dolenjska , Bela Krajina districts. Some 10 million litres are produced here each year even though it is the smallest of the wine producing regions in Slovenia. A wine you are unlikely to find outside Slovenia and popular locally is Cviček from the Dolenjska area.

Primorska

Considering its location adjacent to Italy, the region is probably better developed than the other two regions. Even though Slovenia is a small country, the climactic conditions vary considerable from one side of the country to the other. 25 million litres of wine are produced here each year and among them Brda is probably best known. The Goriška Brda regional climate is Mediterranean, with higher rainfall and moderately hot summers. Kras area produces Teran – but look out for Kras dried ham, too. Also, here are Vipavska Dolina (Malvazija, Rebula, Sauvignon, Beli Pinot, Barbera) and Slovenska Istra (Refošk and Malvazija)

In 2016 wine writer Chris Boiling declared in Wine Tourist Magazine "The Best Country For Wine Tourism? Slovenia" He wrote

> "In the space of a few days and a few hundred miles, I have seen and tasted a vast spectrum of wine. I have tasted some of the best dry white wines in the world – pure expressions of Sauvignon Blanc, Riesling, Pinot Blanc, Pinot Gris, Chardonnay and Traminer. I have tasted their funky variations – Sauvignon Blancs that have been made for aging, Pinot Gris that's pinker than most rosés, Traminers kept in oak barrels for 18 months, and white wines where the grapes have been macerated for more than a year."

And his infectious enthusiasm continued through the reds and the blends and the accommodation too.

[www.winetouristmagazine.com/wt-blog/2016/2/9/the-best-country-for-wine-tourism-slovenia]

Ice Wine

Ice wine is not unique to Slovenia. It is produced in many other countries in the region including Austria, Croatia, Czechia, Denmark, Georgia, France, Hungary, Italy, Lithuania Luxembourg, Poland, Romania, Moldova, Slovakia, Spain, Sweden and Switzerland. Also, in Canada (Ontario is a producer). Some of these countries are not usually associated with wine production.

The grapes for this normally sweet dessert wine have been frozen while on the vine. The water in the grapes freezes, but the sugars don't, leading to producing less juice and a sweet wine which more (sometimes very much more) expensive than ordinary white wine. The harvest is in the winter, even well into January. A good example of ice wine that won't break the bank is Černko Laski Riesling from Jareninsk near Maribor. The 2005 Vintage won a silver award at the San Francisco International Wine Competition in 2006.

Ice wine production is risky (the frost may not come at all before the grapes rot or are otherwise lost) and requires the availability of a large enough labour force to pick the whole crop within a few hours, at a moment's notice, on the first morning that is cold enough. This results in relatively small amounts of ice wine being made worldwide, making ice wines generally quite expensive.

If you enjoy sweet wine, a more recent award – 2015 – in the Decanter World Wine Awards was the Ptujska Klet, Pullus Laski Riesling, 2012. It won and international trophy for sweet wine over £15.

Orange wine

In December 2016, The Independent newspaper carried the headline "Orange wine looks set to be the drink of 2017". That prediction might not have been realised. Orange refers to the colour not the fruit and (just to emphasise the point) is a grape wine. Unlike white wine the skins of white grapes are left with the grape juice to release the tannins. They could be left for weeks or even up to a year. The length of time will produce wines with different looks and flavours. Orange wine probably originated in the Caucasus (modern day Georgia). Production was revitalised by Italian and Slovenian winemakers over the last 20 years, initially in the cross-border Friuli-Venezia Giulia wine and Goriska Brda regions Look out for these producers, Klinec, Movia "Lunar", and Princic.

Local favourites

All the supermarkets and grocery stores have a selection of wines – often the smaller shops have a small but good range.

Shop wine ranges from very cheap (depending on your experience, but certainly in UK terms almost unbelievably cheap). They are rarely expensive. Specialists shops – there are at least three in Bled – will have a more sophisticated range. In the shops and restaurants look out for these names. I can't recommend any one in particular (I am not an expert and I don't know what you like), but these are my order of preference.

White or Red?

My preference at home in red and in Slovenia is white. 75% of Slovenian wine is white. Malvazija, Šipon, and Rebula (Ribolla Gialla in Italy) are my usual picks. The reds you will see in supermarkets are Merlot, Refošk, Cviček, and Teran. I tend to think Teran is something of an acquired taste.

Experiment if you are buying off the shelf in a grocery store. The wine is good and you won't waste your money. In a restaurant ask advice. The Slovenian wait-staff are always proud of Slovenian wine and happy to talk about it.

Where to buy

There are a few specialist wine shops in Bled. My own favourite is Vinoteka Zdravljica where you can sit and try before buying. The staff are lovely and want you to enjoy their wine.

Some people might reserve half a day for the trip around the lake, another a day for the castle, another a day to walk in the hills. I suggest you reserve an afternoon (and possibly the evening) to take a wine tour of Slovenia from a chair at Vinoteka Zdravljica.

Vinoteka Vinarte opposite the Grand Hotel Toplice has limited opening hours; Thursday to Sun from 5:00 pm to 7:00 pm.

There is a tiny wine shop in the main shopping centre.

The cellar in Bled Castle is a unique experience where you can do more than just buy wine – you can learn about viniculture, too.

Zakladi Slovenije or Treasures of Slovenia shop at Cesta svobode 15 is open from 9:00 am to 10:00 pm is a gift shop with a smaller selection of more expensive Slovenian wine.

Wine tourism and wine roads wine routes

The three wine growing regions have been attracting visitors who want to enjoy Slovenia's indigenous cuisine. Again, considering the size of the country there is remarkable variation from the Mediterranean diet of the Istrian coast to the Kranjska Klobasa sausage of Gorenjska area to the stews of Prekmurje in the east.

There are several wine routes suggested by Slovenia Tourism in Prekmurje. The first, Lendava Wine Route, Prekmurje and Goričko Wine Routes. This is white wine country where you will find grape varieties such as Italian Riesling, Chardonnay, Sauvignon, Rhine Riesling, Pinot Blanc, Pinot Gris, Traminer, and Muscatel.

Then there are the Haloze, Ptuj, Ormož, Jeruzalem and Kapela Wine Routes. Two towns to focus on are Ormož and Ptuj, and the vineyards of Jeruzalem and nearby Ljutomer.

Maribor and nearby Pesnica and Podpohorje wine routes have plenty of white wine, but you will also find some reds here such as Pinot Noir, Blue Franconian and Zweigelt.

Then south towards the border with Croatia to Bizeljsko, Dolenjska, and Bela Krajina wine routes. More reds to be found here. In Dolenjska, cviček wine, which is a blend of red Blue Franconian and Žametna črnina varieties with the white Kraljevina and Italian Riesling.

Then towards Italy and Primorska. Vipava Valley's famous reds and whites, then the Karst wine route for kraški teran, and The Istria wine route for Refosco.

Finally, for this very superficial tour, the famous Goriška Brda.

For more details about wine routes and some of the accompanying cuisine see the Slovenia Tourism website.

Wine tasting

Wine tasting in Murka

At 26 years old, Jani Pravdič is a young man-about-town. He partied so much at college that he decided he wanted to make a career having fun and build a business around tourism. And he did, about five years ago, using his social connections and his experience in Ljubljana night life.

He began by taking rich visitors and business people to Ljubljana on VIP tours of the city hot-spots, skipping queues and meeting the right people. On these nightly escapades he noticed the popularity of pub-crawls. He observed that they were popular, but they were not being done the way he would have done them.

Jani likes to get the details right. "I don't drink." This is a surprise. "I take care of the details; the music, the lighting and how to help people enjoy themselves." Jani began the pub crawls just after the recession. Ljubljana nights were quieter the bars less busy, then. He countered that by giving the pub-crawlers a programme of games, entertainment and events at each bar. "Sometimes the pub crawl will attract 100 people a night."

His business evolved into an agency organising stag and hen nights. He kept the pub-crawl but wanted to do something else. "Wine tasting, beer tasting, schnapps tasting. We have tons of small beer makers and so many wine makers, amazing beer, amazing wine. But all the places that were doing the tastings were not doing them on the level I wanted." They were boring, says Jani, and not frequent enough. "I thought: Let's build a wine tasting programme ourselves. With the sommeliers and other wine lovers we created an interactive, fun, short wine tasting course."

The wine tastings are held in two venues. In Ljubljana the events are held in the 200-year-old cellar of Dvorni Bar on Dvorni Trg, near Congress Square. "They learn the basics, they learn about the pairing for food and wine, something of the history and how it is produced." It's a two-hour programme.

In Bled the wine tasters meet in the basement of Gostilna Murka – established more than 100 years ago, it is the second oldest restaurant in Bled. The cellar was originally used for storing ice and now it is the wine cellar. "During the winter the people would take the ice from the lake," and other places, too. "They would store the ice in the basement for the rest of the year."

At both tastings, the group experience wine from all the Slovenian regions. Again, obsessing on the details of the presentation, Jani believes too many wine tastings are just about the wine not about the whole experience of the event. "The people who come to the tastings are from all around the world. They are usually 25 to 60 years old. I had expected we would get a lot of older people, but we get young people as well. We don't attract experts. The people wo come are interested in wine but know virtually nothing – some know a little." He says that his expertise is getting the party just right – ne leaves the tasting to the experts. "I love the idea that they are all interested in the culture of the wines."

In Bled they start around 6 or 7 pm. "We gather in the wine cellar. The sommelier presents 7 wines; red white sparkling. We do it for groups of two to ten. It is cosy, and over the two hours we have fun."

If you want to take part, you should book ahead at Jani's website https://winetastingbled.com/ for Bled and https://winetastingljubljana.com/ for Ljubljana.

Every Thursday at 5:00 pm (May to November) at Hotel Triglav's, wine cellar, there is a guided wine tasting. It lasts an hour or ninety minutes and costs €25. You can get more details from the Hotel Triglav website:

[*www.hoteltriglavbled.si/en/restavracija-1906-bled/vino*]

www.slovenia.si/visit/cuisine/wines/wine-routes/

Some other useful links:

Chris Boiling in Wine Tourist Magazine
www.winetouristmagazine.com/wt-blog/2016/2/9/the-best-country-for-wine-tourism-slovenia

www.jancisrobinson.com/learn/wine-regions/slovenia

www.winetouristmagazine.com/wt-blog/2016/10/15/the-worlds-best-wine-road-jeruzalem-slovenia

www.thinkslovenia.com/info-activities/slovenian-wine

www.decanter.com/decanter-world-wine-awards/dwwa-results-highlights/dwwa-2015-slovenia-win-is-triumph-for-the-underdog-says-mw-262974/

PART 5 –
PEOPLE IN BLED

While the countryside around Bled is beautiful and the lake is "magical" (I did read one reviewer say that it is not "magical enough" and was left thinking about how one measures "magic"), when you get to know some of the people who live there, you really appreciate what makes the town special. Here are a few people I am fortunate to have met. Many more are quoted elsewhere in this book.

Župan (Mayor) of Bled

Profile – Janez Fajfar, the man who represents Bled to the world and at home.

For more than 10 years, Janez Fajfar has been mayor of Bled, the Župan. Apart from his formal duties as the person who runs the town and plans its development, Janez can be seen at almost every event throughout the year, often welcoming tourists and VIPs. Sometimes he even goes back to his teenage years as a tour a tour guide and picks up the microphone to give a commentary as special guests are taken around town.

Professionally and not so co-incidentally his background is in the hospitality industry. Once the manager of Vila Bled, his childhood was spent in the company of other children from abroad when their families stayed with his in rooms rented to tourists.

Always charming, always entertaining, Janez and I have had many long meandering conversations. But for this, to keep us both focused, I asked him to answer a questionnaire. His story is fascinating. He tells us about his past, the many famous people he has met, his hopes for the future and his legacy when he retires.

How long have you been mayor?

Since 2006

What does a mayor do?

It would be much easier to ask what he doesn't do.

With such a long history, are there historic ceremonial duties?

There are no special historic ceremonial duties, but some have been introduced [over the years]. The nicest is the pruning of the castle vine plant, a cutting, a "baby" of a 400 years old vine from Maribor, and cutting of the ripe grapes in autumn, of course.

Do you have duties at the castle, too?

When we have a special guest or just for fun I put on my burgundy coat with the black hare collar and fur cap with a peacock feather and the shiny mayor's chain, of course. Groups from the Far East drop by, all wanting a picture with me and my costume. I have to address numberless delegations and groups and give them a short talk on the past and present of Bled, if possible in a humorous way.

Who are some of the famous and important people you have met?

I am still meeting lots of them. Whenever someone important visits Slovenia, they normally come to Bled, too.

Being a tour guide as a student, then managing the Vila Bled, (Tito's summer residence for 22 years) and now more than 10 years a mayor, I've seen lots of dignitaries. The Queen with Prince Philip, Prince Charles, Prince Edward, just to mention the British, your numerous ministers, like Rifkind, Miliband.

Last year I enjoyed a lot the meeting with Bartholomeus of Constantinople, the world chief of the Eastern Orthodox Church. The most entertaining was the visit of the Spanish royal family, Queen Sofia asked her husband, King Juan Carlos to make a photo. The digital camera just came out, so he was not yet used to it. His royal spouse said to him as any other wife would do: "Is it even this you can't make?"

Mrs. Laura Bush also made a great impression on me, being so well read. Jeff Bridges, William Hurt, Michelle Pfeiffer, Michael Palin, Paul McCartney. Most of them can be really nice people, some cannot. Normally the more import they are, the fewer problems with them.

What did you do before you were mayor?

Before having my present post, I used to run Hotel Vila Bled, once Tito's mansion at the Lake Bled. The government opened it as a hotel four years after Tito's death in 1984. I stared as a reception manager and advanced to the manager in some years. In 1987 Vila Bled was accepted into the nicest hotel chain of the world, Relais & Châteaux. Our clientele was fabulous, very few snobs, mostly good old money, well behaved and respectful. Those who came to show off normally came just once, to the joy of the real ones. The City of London liked us a lot; I was even made a freeman in 2004.

The government rented the place for peanuts to a number of people who had no clue how to run a place like this and I just couldn't stand it anymore and decided to quit in the autumn of 2006. I just wanted to have a break in the winter to learn some of the excellent cooking of my 86 years old mother, retired chef. The municipal elections came in October, some friends finally convinced me to run for mayor and I got it... Now it is my third, four-year term.

Tell us about growing up in Bled

Growing in Bled was nice. We were not rich, but parents got a loan from the municipality to build a rather big home on the condition we rent some rooms to the tourists. I was just six years old when I sold the living room to two Viennese, when my mother was shopping. We had to sleep in the cellar then.

As a child, I could meet many foreign children, we played together and subconsciously learned from each other.

94

Sometimes they would take us with them to Holland for example; they sent us from one to another of the other people coming every year to my home, at the end some one of them would take us along driving to Bled to us, or to one of our neighbours.

Our home was like a railway station, always full of people, coffee, schnapps, salami, cake. Bled as a tourist place, attracted all sorts of people from anywhere. Children found some people to curious, unusual, so we gave remarks and got a slap from the parents.

We liked it a lot when Tito turned up with some exotic president or a royal. The school was out, the teachers sorted us along the main road, we got one of those colourful paper flags to wave when the endless line of the limousines passed by. The handles of the flags were the best materials for arrows for our cowboy and Indians battles.

What did your parents do?

We were a family of five; I was the middle one of three children. My mother was a magician of a chef. In the sixties and seventies guests were staying at our home on full board. We served about twenty people, also some tourists staying with our neighbours. So many dishes to wash and dry. My father was a mechanic, really widely known. He was always dressed in his blue overall, liked the cognac too much. Anyhow, police left him in peace, because they needed him more as he needed them. Both parents were good in several languages, something rather normal in a tourist place...

What are some of the best things about Bled?

The best thing is just to make an early morning or an evening walk the six kilometres around the lake, depend less of the weather or the season.

Do you have a favourite legend?

Definitely the legend of the sunken bell. (You can read about it later in the book.)

How many languages do you speak?

Next to the native Slovenian, practised by just two million people, I learned the Serbo-Croatian; we started to learn English at school with eleven years. I picked up Italian and German from or guests, specially their children. I learned quite good French at the college, Polish as a side subject at University and some Spanish. I picked up Dutch as a tour guide on the bus.

When did you start learning languages?

I was always keen of music and wanted to understand what they sing. Being all the season with lots of foreign children, I learned the most of them.

What would you like to see happening in Bled in the future?

To be a bit political at the end: my first wish is for both very necessary bypass roads, the northern and the southern, they'll push the traffic away from lake. This will be the basis for an even better level of the tourists coming to Bled.

I'll do my best to keep Bled green and respecting our enormous natural and cultural heritage. I would also like to make Bled as good for our citizens as for the foreigners.

What is the best thing you can do or see in Bled that tourists usually miss? What is the insider's secret about Bled?

Walking or taking a buggy ride through the nearby villages, climbing up Osojnica for the incredible view. Triglav National Park Information Centre.

Domen Kalajžič – Founder of 3glav Adventures

As you walk up the hill out of Bled along Ljubljanska cesta, on your left there is a small green shack. It is filled with the stuff of adventures. It attracts your attention because it looks a little out of place, perhaps a little out of time. It belongs here, but did it come from somewhere else? There is nothing like it in Bled.

A hundred years ago it was a tailor's shop belonging to the King's tailor. The Kingdom of the Serbs, Croats and Slovenians was founded in 1918 and the royal family had a summer palace where Vila Bled is situated. The little green shack is the place where the tailor's great grandson Domen Kalajžič runs 3glav Adventures.

3glav (or Triglav) is named after the highest mountain in Slovenia. You can see its peaks from Bled if you look to the west.

"It was at the old Bled Lesce train station before the first world war." Domen tells me. "My great-grandfather bought the ticket office when they built the proper brick train station in Lesce. He bought the hut and somehow transported it to Bled and put it where 3glav Adventures office now is. The building where it stands now protected. It is more than 200 years old and has been in Domen's family for 100 years."

The humble green wooden structure is as much part of Bled's history as any palace. It was passed from generation to generation. "Four or five generations now. Usually the same business passes from one generation to another, but this little green hut has served our family for totally different types of businesses in each generation." First a tailor's, then Domen's mother ran a herbal pharmacy. Now an adventure business.

Domen is the first generation of adventurers. Three years after Slovenia became an independent nation in 1991, Domen began travelling. It was a gap year between high school and university. "It was the new age of back packing – the pioneering years. Economically it was pretty hard. Air tickets

97

were a lot more expensive. I had travelled before, but this was my first serious trip."

Aged 18, free for four or five months, Domen first headed south to Australia and New Zealand. It was the beginning of a way of life. Every year since then he has spent four or five months travelling.

That's where he got the travel bug, but the idea for running a tourist adventure business had not even begun to form in his mind. Domen's focus was still on travel. When he graduated from university in 1999 with a degree in Information Technology & Management, the world was his to explore and he spent a whole year discovering it.

Yet, there were no thoughts about starting a tourism business. He settled in America for three years, "I was in California from 2000 to 2003 running a small computer company named Brainworks. Of course, in my free time I was exploring Santa Monica mountains and other outdoor areas every weekend by mountain bike or hiking. I know North America pretty well and I keep returning every year since 1996 doing local road trips and hiking in the less known regions. The great outdoors there are magnificent, on contrary of what our parents here in Slovenia always told us, that in America, there's just concrete, a concrete jungle.

"It was the best time to be in the IT business in Los Angeles. I started my computer company there, it was great fun. All Slovenians have a strong connection to the outdoors. Our parents take us to the mountains at the weekends. We hiked in California and still travelled as much as I could from there. But then I got a bit homesick. I came back one summer, and I just stayed."

Bled, the mountains, the outdoors were the perfect base for Domen and having settled home worked with a friend in the mountain bike business for a year.

"For 10 years, from 1994 to 2004, with all my travellers and all the locals I clicked with and had great times with I kept on inviting everyone to my beautiful country expecting that maybe one out of ten might come. Eventually almost everyone I invited came from all over the world." His parent's house – next to the green shack – turned into an unofficial hostel. "People kept coming and my parents made them breakfasts and I was taking them around. I really enjoyed it – it was my hobby next to work. There were people from all over the world staying with us and I am so thankful to my parents – they were non-payed hostel operators."

Here was the beginning of the idea. People kept on coming and Domen was very proud to show them the best of his country and this beautiful region of Gorenjska (Upper Carniola). He had bought an old Chrysler Voyager, a luxury mini-van with six seats plus a driver.

"A friend was managing Bledec Hostel." Then, from the start of 2000s until 2006, it was the only hostel in Bled right at the top of the hill in the old town, beneath the castle. It is still a popular place at Grajska cesta 17. "She told me that the young people or active people who come to Bled get bored after two days seeing the island, the castle and of course Vintgar. And then they don't know what to do."

He had the van and a fulltime job in the mountain bike business. "I connected the dots from all the places my friends who visited over the last ten years liked the most, to our main adventure, the Emerald River Adventure." He created a full day trip from Bled all around the Triglav National Park and Julian Alps.

"Every evening after work, I went to the hostel and I presented the trip to the travellers there." Starting slowly, one traveller then two, by the end of the season he had five in the mini-van taking the first version of the Emerald River Adventure.

After the summer he made the big decision. He quit his "real" job. "And no matter what happens," He said. "That's what I really want to do."

The only resources Domen had were the van and some brochures. The shack was still his mother's apothecary business. Around the same time, she decided to retire. "They

99

wanted to rent the place, but I said, no, I want to try something new."

It was a slow start – but Domen saw that tourism was changing. People were drifting away from the beach holiday, lying in the sun doing nothing, and were engaging in healthier more adventurous holidays.

This is when the 3glav Emerald River Adventure began. They still run today. "It's a great introduction to the greater area around Bled; Triglav National Park and Julian Alps. It starts at 8 o'clock in the morning from Bled. It's a road trip by minivan with up to 8 people plus our guide. We do a loop through Kranjska Gora, Jasna Lake, and make the first hike – around 45 minutes – at the top of Vršič where they get great 360-degree views of the Julian Alps."

Kranjska Gora is a beautiful alpine town a few kilometres from Italy in one direction and Austria in another direction. Skiing is the main sport in the winter with spectacular scenic walks and driving tours during the rest of the year. High above is Vršič – "the Russian Road" – the highest mountain pass in Slovenia at 1611 meters altitude and was built by Russian prisoners of war in the 1st world war.

"Sometimes we stop at the Russian Chapel." Domen tells me. "It depends on the group and their interests. There is a world war 1 museum in Kobarid."

Kobarid Museum displays exhibits on the events that occurred during World War 1 on the Soška fronta - Isonzo Front. "The biggest mountain battle in history, unfortunately. Ernest Hemmingway wrote "Farewell to Arms" here. He was one of the soldiers."

The Emerald River Adventure brings people to lesser known places – off the beaten path – in Triglav National Park. There are three 45-minute walks. The next hike is to the source of the Soča. "Then everybody meets the Soča from the very start, and then we spend most of the day all the way along the river. Most people do the optional rafting in Bovec. And then we take another hike to the most amazing Kozjak waterfall."

The trip continues through Kobarid and close to Tolmin the mini-van is put on a train for the next part of the journey to Bohinj. "You sit in the van on the train and there is a 45-minute fun ride."

The day finishes in Bohinj and then back to Bled.

The adventure attracts all sorts of people from 18 to 75, and families too. I asked Domen about older people, people who have worked in an office all their lives, now retired and enjoying the beauty of Slovenia. How do they cope with the adventure? "We don't consider anything we do as extreme." He says. "All our adventures are like any Slovenian spending their time outdoors. We put safety first but don't do anything intensive. They are just nice getaways to the great outdoors. Everyone should be at least moderately fit. It's not suitable for someone who doesn't like nature. Age doesn't matter."

There are likely to be people from all over the world in any group of eight who are together for one day only. The bonding of those people is one of the things that makes this trip the most interesting.

When tourism is well managed, it can be a great boon to a country or region. Paradoxically, where the environment is fragile, and the balance of nature is the very thing that attracts visitors, tourism can be damaging. That which people come to see, can be destroyed by the people who love it. Over the last four or five years, Slovenia Tourism, Visit Ljubljana and Bled Tourism have worked tirelessly promoting the country. In 2017 there were several international publications pointing to Slovenia – and Lake Bled, the jewel in Slovenia's crown – as the place to visit in 2018. Domen and I discussed his concerns about the pressures tourism puts on the region.

"Slovenia was under the radar until about five years ago. I think with the popularity in the last five years, we should be careful what kind of tourism strategy we shall have in the future. Slovenia is a very small country and it is fragile. I've noticed Bled doesn't have the infrastructure to cope with masses of people visiting in the last three years. The Slovenian Tourism Organisation and all of us should sit down and discuss the future of tourism here. We should focus and specialise in something."

Domen still spends several months of the year travelling to other parts of the world. "I love all the places around the world, really - everywhere is beautiful and just different. You can find beauty in the people everywhere as you can find beauty in nature everywhere, even in the sand desert. Favourites are Northern Thailand, Morocco and Saharan countries, South Africa, Japan. Diversity of cultures and nature is what I like - sometimes differences are so distinctive and pronounced that seems like jumping from one planet to another one."

Domen is keenly aware of the effect tourism can have on the nature his tours celebrate. He looks forward to the time that Bled serves, "Respectful tourists who appreciate what we have. 3glav Adventures takes tourists to nature in Triglav National Park, but we are trying to respect and protect our nature as much as possible. And we do. It's in our blood.

"When you travel through Slovenia there's almost no trash or litter anywhere. That's a positive sign, because I visited Belgrade a few days ago and it reminded me of Slovenia in the time of Yugoslavia. It was littered with trash all over the country. Since we got independence everyone has an awareness of preserving our country as much as possible. I'm really proud I can consider my country and my town pretty clean."

The Emerald River Adventure is just one of the 3glav Adventures programmes. There is a variety to suit various levels of experience. From river adventures to balloon trips even skydiving.

"For us the best reward is happy people and then, we are happy as well."

3glav Adventures specialises in summer activities and is open from mid-April to mid-October.

Address: Ljubljanska cesta 1, 4260 Bled, Slovenia

Phone: +386 41 683 184

Web: www.3glav.com/

Insider Knowledge:

My few hours crazy busy summer escape alone is to a little hidden gorge 300-400 meters from Lake Bohinj down the Sava Bohinjka river stream. It's a really hidden corner – so I am going to keep its whereabouts a secret. (Hint: if you explore some of the paths and walks near Bohinj Hotel you might find it.)

Our favourite short family escape with our 6 and 8 years old kids is only 10-15 mins drive away from Bled - a "hidden" lake Završnica located at the trail-head for Mt. Stol, beautiful area below Karavanke mountain range that is amazing outdoor playground away from crowds even in peak summer months.

Domen Kalajžič

Jernej Brence, Founder and Director Festival Bled

Over two weeks during the summer, there will be concerts by established musicians, performances by young music students who have been attending masterclasses, and other events in several venues around the town.

This is will be the 23rd festival which was established by Jernej Brence. Jernej is a quiet, unassuming character who you will see at every performance. But no brash impresario he. Attracting little attention, as he stands with friends in a corner or at a doorway or sitting at the edge of the audience appreciating the music. Yet it is by force of personality that this festival of music and arts has lasted so long.

I asked Jernej to reflect on the previous 22 years.

What was it like growing up in Bled?

Growing up on the shores of Lake Bled was pure poetry for a child. The mountains, lakes, forests and in particular, life on the Alpine foothills. Later, that was also the biggest reason why I was looking for the first opportunity to return home from Vienna.

Do you come from a musical family?

I do not know. But I know that my uncle Davorin Brence, who died in 1943 in the Second World War, left the family 3 violins. As a small child, I examined one in detail, and in particular the interior, the second, I sent downstream as a boat. The third, my mother decided I should use to learn to play.

I later found notes of my uncle's fingering which (from a present day perspective) for his age (he died at the age of 17) is straightforwardly genius. Older people who knew him say that I am very similar to him. Perhaps in a sense a reincarnation?

Only the most gifted children go from learning an instrument to studying and playing as professionals. When did people realise you had a real talent?

The family has a great influence. Some children do it for their parents, some are given the option, and for some it is instinct. A real educator recognises the instinct ...

How did that affect your life and school?

A lot. I do not want to claim that I had no problems learning to play the violin as a student. Later, as a teacher, you see a whole range of problems that you had not had yourself, but you experience them along with the students. It is also the other way around, namely, that you also learn something from your students.

You studied in Vienna with Prof. Michael Frischenschlager. Was that your first time away from home? How was that experience? I went to Vienna to study. It was not my first long trip from home, because before that I had served a 15-month military service in the YPA [the Yugoslav army], where I met people of all nationalities from the former Yugoslavia. Vienna was "cultural shock" for me. Parks, in which bushes are sheared "with a ruler", the discipline they demanded from us, genius classmates who came from all over the world (barely a tenth of them were from Austria).

How did the Festival begin?

And so this is how Festival Bled was created. After the war of Independence, nobody much ventured to Bled because the foreign media reported for years afterwards that the war was still going. But my professor Michael Frischenschlager and classmates were not firghtened. Because I was a little older, I was already independent and could have been teaching violin, I was hoping to invite my entire class with my professor to Bled (with my mother's help, I should add). We started off with a musical cast that you could not have seen anywhere else. Patricija Kopačinskaja from Moldova, Giovanni Angeleri from Italy, Christian Nenescu from Romania, Mario Hossen from Bulgaria, Iljija Marinkovič from Serbia, Nahu Uemura from Japan, Sandor Javorkai from Hungary, Xiang Chen from China. They performed thematic evenings, music by Paganini, Mozart, J.S. Bach. And so that is how Festival Bled was created and it was named VIOLIN. Later, when the festival expanded, many of the glittering names were discovered and heard in the Masterclass courses at Bled. People like Piotr Jasiurkovsky, Maxim Brylinsky, Tymur Meljnik, Valentin Eichler. At the same time, Slovenian students had the opportunity to measure up to their standards and acquaint themselves with them, which has resulted in the rise in Slovenian student participants. Let me just mention Iztok Hrastnik (double bass) and my pupil Petro Kovačič, who are both permanent members of the Vienna Philharmonic.

How do you think the Festival will develop in the future?

During its 22 years, the Bled Festival has become a place to find talented players of all sorts of music; classical, jazz, rock, crossover. We will always keep the Masterclass courses which in no small way form an important part of the Festival. Regardless of the music genre, we are seeking quality for the evening concerts. They are our speciality but concerts represent only half of the events in the Festival. The rest are painting exhibitions, jam session, and this year we are introducing evenings of poetry.

And, above all, we realize that success comes with love, but never without it.

Festival Bled 2018 will be held 2 to 14 July at various venues in Bled. Check www.festivalbled.com for listings and details.

Jernej answered the questions in Slovenian. Here are his words untranslated.

What was it like growing up in Bled?

Odraščanje na Bledu je bilo meni kot otroku čista poezija. Gore, jezera, gozd in specifika predalpskega življenja .... To je bil največji razlog, da sem iskal prvo možnost, da se z Dunaja vrnem domov.

Do you come from a musical family?

Ne vem. Vem pa, da je moj stric Davorin Brence, ki je umrl leta 1943 v drugi svetovni vojni, zapustil družini 3 violine. Kot majhen otrok sem eno podrobno pregledal tudi in predvsem v notranjosti, drugo poslalkot ladjico po potočku, na tretjo sem se pa po odločitvi moje mame moral naučiti igrati .... Kasneje sem našel še note s stričevimi prstnimi redi, ki so bili (iz sedanjega vidika) za njegovo starost (umrl je s 17. leti!) naravnost genialni. Starejši ljudje, ki so ga poznali, pravijo, da sem mu zelo podoben. Morda v nekem smislu reinkarnacija ?

Only the most gifted children go from learning an instrument to studying and playing as professionals. When did people realise you had a real talent?

Velik vpliv ima družina. Nekateri otroci gredo zaradi staršev, nekateri dobijo možnost, nekaterim pa je to nagon. Pravi pedagog spozna nagon ...

How did that affect your life and school?
Zelo. Nočem trditi, da pri igranju učenju violine kot študent nisem imel problemov. Kasneje imš kot pedagog celo paleto težav, ki jih osebno nisi nikoli imel, temveč jih prevzameš od študentov. Je pa tudi obratno, namreč da se od učencev tudi nekaj naučiš.

You studied in Vienna with Prof. Michael Frischenschlager. Was that your first time away from home? How was that experience?

Študirat sem šel na Dunaj.To ni bil moj prvi daljši izlet od doma, kajti prej sem odslužil 15 mesečni vojaški rok v JLA, kjer sem spoznal ljudi vseh narodnosti bivše jugoslavije. Dunaj je bil zame » kulturni šok«. Parki, v katerih so še grmovja ostrižena »z ravnilom«, disciplina, ki so jo zahtevali od nas, genialni sošolci, ki so prihajali iz vsega sveta (Avstrijcev je bila komaj desetina).

How did the Festival begin?

In prav tako je nastal Festival Bled. Po osamosvojitvi SLO nihce ni upal na Bled, ker so mediji (tuji) poročali, da je tu vojna še nekaj let za tem. Bali pa se niso moj prof. Michael Frischenschlager in sošolci. Ker sem bil nekoliko starejši, sem bil že samostojen in sem pučeval violino, sem si upal povabiti ves razred s profesorjem vred (moram omeniti, da s podporo moje mame) na Bled, kjer smo potem poceli stvari, ki jih ne vidis nikjer in zasedbo ,ki jo tudi ne srecac zlahka na kupu: Patricija Kopačinskaja-moldavija, Giovanni angeleri- Italija, Christian Nenescu- Romunija, Mario Hossen- Bolgarija, Iljija Marinkovič- Srbija, Nahu Uemura- japonska, Sandor Javorkai-Madžarska, Xiang Chen – Kitajska; so izvajali tematične večere: Paganini, Mozart, J.S. Bach...... Tako je nastal Festival Bled, ki se ga je prijelo ime VIOLINA. Kasneje, ko se je festival širil, smo v okviru mojstrskih tečajev na Bedu odkrili in slišali še veliko dane blestečih imen: Piotr Jasiurkovsky, Maxim Brylinsky, Tymur Meljnik, valentin Eichler.... hkrati pa so imeli slovenski študentje možnost pomeriti in spoprijateljiti se z njimi, kar je prineslo vzgon v slovenskih študentskih vrstah. Naj omenim samo Iztoka Hrastnika (kontrabas) in mojo učenko Petro Kovačič, ki sta oba stalna člana Dunajskih filharmonikov.

How do you think the Festival will develop in the future?

Festival Bled se je v 22 letih razvil kot iskalec talentov vseh stilov glasbe (klasika, jazz, rock, cross over..) zaradi česar bo tudi obdržal mojstrske tečaje- ne nazadnje je iz njih tudi nastal. Išče kvaliteto ne glede na žanr v svojih večernih koncertih. Je pa posebnost v svetu, ker koncerti predstavljajo samo polovico dogajanja, ostalo so slikarske razstave, jam sessioni, letos pa uvajamo še večere poezij. In predvsem se zavedamo, da uspeh pride z ljubeznijo, nikoli pa ne brez nje.

Jernej Slivnik, General Secretary Bled Rowing

Bled Rowing Club has hosted local, national and international regattas for decades. The history of rowing here may well go back centuries. Many rowers from Bled have represented Slovenia at the Olympics and other elite sporting events around the world. The town is twinned with Henley-on-Thames in England, once the home of the Oxford and Cambridge Boat Race and since 1839, the venue for the Henley Royal Regatta.

On a typical sunny afternoon all is quiet around the Rowing Centre until the regattas begin and then it is a centre of activity and excitement. On a walk or cycle around the lake, you will pass the Rowing Centre, the renovated building now houses a restaurant and café and there is room to sit outside and enjoy beautiful views and other facilities like bike hire. "It's open to the public all the time, except the boathouse and the gym," says Jernej Slivnik. The restaurant is owned by Rowing Bled, but it is run by hospitality professionals. "There are three sections. One is the bar, then there is the restaurant offering food and drinks, there are also rooms for guests. I think there are 40 beds," he continues. "We try to accommodate our athletes from other parts of Slovenia when they are here at training camps, otherwise they are normal tourist rooms. There is a small tennis court next to the facilities. We are trying to connect all the partners and to host rowing teams from all around the world to enable them to have training here and for us to get some funds for the club."

Jernej Slivnik is fulltime Secretary General of the Slovenian Rowing Federation (Veslaška zveza Slovenije), the governing body for the sport in the country. He was appointed in 2009 after university and having been a young athlete. He was a rower in the 1990s as a junior and under 23. After attending university he returned to the rowing club, first as an announcer at the regattas then Secretary General. Then he became a member of the managing board of the rowing club and is now co-executive director of the organizing committee which deals with all the major rowing events in Bled.

Formed in 1952, the Federation is responsible for Slovenia's national rowing team, and organising international regattas. Bled has hosted four World Rowing Championships in 1966, 1979, 1989 and 2011, and two World Cup regattas, in 2011 and 2015. The club has produced world-class rowers and Olympic medallists, including Iztok Čop, Luka Špik, Sadik Mujkič, Jani Klemenčič, Denis Žvegelj, Bojan Prešeren and Milan Janša.

Rowing is Jernej's life. This father and brothers were rowers and his home is close to the Centre. "I actually started as a coxswain in 1990. I was a member of the Yugoslav cox four in Tasmania world championship. I have been to two junior world rowing championships the last one was in Strathclyde in Scotland in '96. I'm still an active rower"

Between 1962 and 1964, the rowing team were particularly successful. They had their "famous eight" coming fourth in the Tokyo Olympics. All eight members of the team were from Bled rowing club. "That was the first competitive peak for Bled rowing, because when we talk about Slovenia rowing we are talking about Bled rowing. Not Yugoslavia, of course, as there were other centres like Belgrade and Split."

When the world championships were held in 1966 the infrastructure was improved further and again in 1979. By the time the rowing world championships were next held in Bled in 1989, there were more improvements to the facilities and the to the lake. The town itself was going through a renewal. The shopping centre (known locally as a Gadaffi centre) was opened and the main road into Bled was imported. For the athletes there was reward, too with a bronze medal for the cox pair.

You need to go back to the generation before both Jernej and his brother became involved in the sport to find the beginnings of modern rowing in Bled. It began with his father who was born in the house next to the rowing club. He too began as a coxswain before becoming rower. In the 1970s he began managing the club with Miloš Janša who represented Yugoslavia in the 1972 Munch Olympics in the coxless four.

Following the successes in the 1960s the club had fallen into something of a decline over the next decade.

Jernej's father and Miloš Janša began a new era of Bled Rowing by guiding the team to win medals, first in the junior level then later, the first senior medal was won at the Seoul Olympics in 1988 going on to further wins at Barcelona in 1972. "At first, they were both coaches, then my father took a more administrative and management duties while Miloš focused his work as a coach. Then after the independence of Slovenia he became the Secretary General of the Federation."

1955 for the 1956 European rowing championships. They were the first big event in Bled."

Jernej went on to explain that while the lake is very beautiful now, after the Second World War it wasn't maintained properly. The concentration of efforts was at the town, or eastern side of the lake. The west side became wild and overgrown. The infrastructure that we can see now was not built and the finishing line was yet to be moved from the town side to where it is now. It has been around where they now have the starting point for races. But those changes could not be undertaken until the course was extended and the western side of the lake developed properly.

Before then the course was shorter, not the 2000 metres it is now. Once again, the main changes came about in the 1950s. "To create the finishing area, they had to dig out the last part of the course. So now that we have 2120 metres which allows for the big events; the 2000 metres plus 120 metres to slow down and stop.

"In the fifties everything began with the establishment of the rowing club and the new location which was now in the Mala Zaka bay where all of the facilities are now located. That includes the boathouse the gym the restaurant and it continued to develop.

"We had three world championships; 1966, 1979, and 1989, The last one in 2011 when the centre was fully renovated. "

The 1956 world championships established the club, and the boat house was built then. Bled Rowing was very well supported by politicians during the communist era and the president of the rowing federation Boris Kocijančič was well established in Yugoslav politics. His son Janez Kocijančič became the president of the long-time President of the Slovenian Olympic Committee. Investments were made in the sport and funds were available for the club to build the centre and to support athletes.

The 1989 championship marked the turnaround in Bled Rowing fortunes and the path to the 1992 Barcelona Olympics leading to further success in Sydney. "The from the 90s to the early 2000s was the biggest peak, for Bled Rowing and Slovenian Rowing, after the independence. Iztok Čop and Luka Špik won two medals in the Barcellona Olympics and Čop became the world champion in the single skull in 95 and Luka and Iztok became world champions in '99. Together they were Olympic campions in Sydney in 2000.

"But I think there were two mistakes at that time. The people running Slovenian Rowing, the coaches and the managers, forgot about the youngsters. They were concentrating on the winners and not paying enough attention to the people coming afterwards – the people who would win the next series of medals. Everything was concentrated on the big guys, all the fans were supporting them, and then in 2009 and 2010 we had no youngsters replacing those who had finished their careers, and this had a big impact not just on Bled Rowing, but on other clubs which were developing with Bled. We still feel the consequences now. We have no competitive athletes at all – we can't reach the finals or the semi-finals of the big events. So, when you hit the bottom, which I think we hit in 2013 and 2014, it's hard to come back. There is a motivation problem for the athletes and the coaches." It was the first hint on pessimism in Jernej's voice. But only for a moment.

"I believe we are now back on track because Iztok Cop finished his competitive career after the London Olympics, this was the last medal at the big events for Slovenia. After some time off, he has returned to rowing and has been very active in the

Olympic Committee. Last year we agreed to have him as a head coach of the Slovenian Rowing team and things are now happening. He is the right person to do it because of what he has achieved."

He's also a good name to attract people, I suggested. "Yes, he is a role model for the future – this is the key. We have been concentrating on the youngsters and we have won the bid for the 2020 World Championships for the Juniors and the Under 23s here in Bled. And we are presenting these championships as a big step towards building careers. This is the main project of the federation and the club."

The 2011 world championships brought further renovation of the Centre. "At last – it was in a really bad state. We managed to attract some European funds. Also, the president of the Federation in 2009 was Denis Žvegelj one of the medallists from Barcelona. I became the Secretary General, and this developed into a very good organising committee able to organise any event in world rowing. We had 2010 world cup, 2011 world championships, 2012 European rowing junior championships, 2015 World Cup and in 2017 world rowing masters regatta which was a record breaking rowing event ... biggest ever in the FISA family."

In 2018, for the 63rd year, Bled hosts traditional Annual International Regatta from 15th to 17th June. "This is a very good regatta for the juniors and under 23s It attracts 600 athletes from 50 nations. We will be hosting the best crews from middle and eastern Europe. Every year we host the first national regatta usually at the end of April. We call it the First of May Regatta; it is more or less, the national trials. Then it's the Youth Challenge Regatta for under 16s and under 14s. It's for the youngsters so it's only 1000 meters. We are joining it with the Masters – we are trying to get some Masters to return to Bled and compete here. Then the International Regatta in June. Then the traditional national annual championships held each year in Lake Bled. It's the only regular rowing course in Slovenia This will be the 27th edition of the National Championships."

Bled is twinned with Henley on Thames, and there are plans for further collaboration with Henley Rowing Club. "We have been to their regattas, they have been to Bled regattas in the past and now we are talking to Upper Thames Rowing Club to exchange once again. So, we will probably be going to a regatta there in August (2018) and they will be coming to one of our regattas. This is one of the things we are very proud of."

From seeing mistakes in the past, Jernej realises that it's all well and good to celebrate the present, but the future successes are in the planning of events and bringing forward young talent. They are looking at least 10 years into the future. "We are focusing on 2020 World Championships. This will be for non-Olympic events for the Seniors, Under 23s and the Juniors. And our plan is to bid and win the bid for the 2023 European Championships. And we are planning to bid for the World Rowing Championships in 2027 or perhaps the year before or after.

Have all those activities on the water, the rowing, the racing, attracting people from around the world, have they had a positive impact on the lake? "Definitely. It keeps the lake in shape. We look after the infrastructure, the banks of the lake. We manage the start and the finish areas, also the rowing centre, altogether that is quite a big part of the whole lake."

Walking among the fans and athletes on a summer's day, either at the Rowing Centre, or the finishing line, or at several other viewpoints on the lake shore, you soak up a sporting, the competitive, the celebratory atmosphere. "The big events attract a lot of people, first the teams then the spectators who come to see the events. In world rowing family now, we have a very good status. We are the only one - along with Lucerne - to host the four world championships."

Insider knowledge.

"Our partner hotel has a good restaurant – Hotel Astoria. That's where we hold all our meetings and congresses and that's where we accommodate the athletes from other Slovenian rowing clubs. They are very friendly to the athletes and they think it is the best hotel in Bled. They offer proper

food for sportsmen. They also have a very good gym and it's a good place to relax.

"We also collaborate very well with Hotel Triglav which is quite near to the rowing centre where we accommodate the VIPs usually FISA members. In 2011 during the World Championship we had our national team there. The restaurant tries to develop Slovenian cuisine – which I think is very good. All the ingredients are from local farmers, Also, there are some very good wines from the Slovenian wine regions. I think it is the top facility in Bled.

"Sometimes we have corporate rowing events – training events emphasising teamwork through rowing. It's about co-operation and synchrony Then after the rowing we go to the Triglav to have culinary training there which also emphasises team work.

When Jernej gets time to escape the hustle and bustle of Bled, does he have any secret destinations the heads for? Perhaps it's no surprise he finds peace at the other nearby lake. He goes to Lake Bohinj. "Friends and people are very nice. In my opinion it is more beautiful. It's quiet, Autumn and spring are the best time to go."

His second choice for a place to have time to himself is Pokljuka – the forests and the quietness and during the winter, the cross-country skiing.

Jernej Slivnik

You can keep up to date with news about Bled Rowing at their website www.veslaska-zveza.si/author/jernej/

Ana Pirih – Yoga Bled

Interview with Ana Pirih, founder, teacher and organiser Yoga Bled

When, more than 160 years ago a Swiss natural healer Arnold Rikli came to visit Bled for the first time he noted the curative effect of the environment; the air, the water and the climate. He may not have been the first person to appreciate the healthy surroundings – the town has a history of natural apothecaries, and there are still some who live there – but he was the first to create tourism around the idea of seeking a healthy lifestyle.

In 1895 he built a hospital and outdoor wooden "huts" exposed to the elements where people would stay to regain their health. Word spread, and people came from throughout Europe to find a cure.

Bled has a history and tradition of healthy living and people come for the air and the activities. Among them and added more recently, is outdoor yoga founded by a young woman, Ana Pirih, who is a radio presenter and TV host, journalist and freelance presenter.

"I teach vinyasa flow yoga, I meditate, I am still on stage presenting for an audience. There are so many things that I like to study or to research but every day I am a yoga teacher."

When Pop-Up Yoga Bled began in 2015, Ana was a student of the art. She had only begun practising. Now, Yoga Bled is a permanent feature of the summer at the lake. "What attracted me to yoga was the peacefulness that I got at the end of the practice."

In the early morning, sometimes in the evening, if you are strolling around Lake Bled, you are likely to see a group of people immersed in concentration, eyes closed, bodies stretched. It is as likely as not to be a popup yoga session organised by Ana.

"I remember my first yoga session. I remember driving home. I usually drive with the music up loud, but this time I had such a peaceful smile on my face, and I really enjoyed the silence and everything that was happening around me. It is being in the moment – and that was the most beautiful thing that I felt. That drew me into wanting to know more about yoga and wanting to try more. So, I started practicing every day. And every day it brought me even more of that peacefulness. What was most interesting is how I slowly started to get deeper feelings about myself and how I feel inside, not just the physical part, but the emotional part and my breathing and how that is all connected."

The pop-up sessions are open to anyone and held several times a week – check the Facebook page for details (see below). "Vinyasa is one of the many types of yoga. Vinyasa flow is a bit more dynamic. Hatha is a little slower – Vinyasa is much more connected to the integration of the breath and movement of the body. And asanas (the postures) are a bit more challenging. But it's OK for everybody from beginners to advanced yogis."

Ana had been practising meditation for several years and yoga for about a year before starting Yoga Bled. After first year of Yoga Bled, she applied for teacher training. "The first year Maruša thought all of the classes. I didn't want to teach yet, before I got all the schooling needed to teach.

The project sprung from a spontaneous idea. "It was not – 'Oh, this is what I'm going to do, and this is the plan.'" Ana was sitting at home writing in her journal. It was a habit to record her thoughts and ideas or as she calls them her intentions, "They are little wishes, manifestations of what I want to do. At that time, I was already practising yoga – just by myself. And I started writing a programme for yoga. I wrote pages and pages. I basically wrote what I wanted to create for people at Lake Bled, and how I want to connect yoga with that."

She called her first yoga teacher Maruša to ask her if she would become involved. It was late winter when they met at a café beside the lake. Maruša greeted the idea enthusiastically. "

'This is crazy – yes of course.' She said. We sat down in the café where they sell cream cake, it was late winter, we were sitting outside talking about how we could make this idea a reality. We had a little bit of money, very little though compared to what was written there in the journal. We just had this big insane wish to follow the intentions that I had written. And I said why don't we just do yoga rather than all the other things I had written in my journal? And I said "Maruša, why not Pop Up Yoga Bled? We tell people a week before where we are going to be. Let's do that to begin."

"She has this amazing energy. When she is enthusiastic she is really enthusiastic, and she shouts "Yes! Let's do this!" I started emailing people from the hotels to ask if we can practice in their parks, and everything just fell together from 2014 to 2015. I still get Goosebumps when I think about that."

She compares the calm she got from meditation with the calm she experiences following a yoga session. "It's like after 20 minutes of meditation when you are sitting in a forest. You don't think about "Oh, I have this and that to do. I need to this with my project. Oh, how much money I have – I have to earn blah, blah, blah" You are just here. Or sometimes when you have so much fun with your friends, I could compare it to the feelings you have when you are with your friends or your loved ones when you simply forget about time and the spontaneity just grows."

Ana says yoga lead her to finding who she is "But that doesn't happen the first year, or even the second," for her, it came after the teacher training. "When I began to realise that there were a lot of things that I have built around me that I didn't want to show to myself or others. It was the deep practice. Now I understand the meaning of practice, practice, practice. Because if you don't do the work of self-reflection, you don't come to yourself."

Yoga Bled can pop up anywhere around the lake. Ana says that she wanted to connect the whole place together. "This is not my activity, my yoga studio, the only place you can find me. We wanted to connect all of the places together and by this make people feel the presence of the location such as parks and how much the location can give you. When you are not inside a yoga studio, but outside, amazing things happen. We get animals bumping into the practice session because they somehow feel the energy. You really get to feel the life of the place. At the end of the practice when you get that feeling of peacefulness, you can really sense everything around you. When I see people sit down in a quiet place I let them be there and sometimes we stay there for an hour – even more. We talk and hang out because amazing energy gets to rise up. and that's the most beautiful reward you can get."

Most of the people who attend the Yoga Bled sessions are in their 20s, some are older and there are no limitations who can attend. "And this was part of my quiet wish intention. I wanted to bring yoga to young people because it can give you so much growth that you can start practicing it can help you grow from the inside. And they come from all over the world."

She gets a lot of people on holiday and want to try something new. "Also, people who are in search of quietness, who just want to calm down, I get people who are working a lot and they contact me because their doctor told them they needed to practice, and they are on vacation and have time. I talk to them about how they can put practice into their schedule back home. They get a little bit of a souvenir here; Yoga Bled at Lake Bled, which is not something you can grab with your fingers, but you can really take that into your heart and maybe try it for yourself back home."

Ana has also studied Arnold Rikli the Swiss natural healer. "He came here because he had problems with his health and he was searching for a place where he could get better. And he felt the energy here. And he got better and then – a little like I did – he got inspired by this and he created something for everyone. He started the Rikli Centre where he also built huts where people stayed and here he helped people get better with the sun, the water and the air.

"He treated people with what Lake Bled offers – the sunlight the fresh water the fresh air and people were sun bathing, naked if they wanted and swimming naked in the water, our natural costume. They were walking barefoot – he knew back then this was good for the body, it's good for the posture. And people really got better when they were here at his centre. Nature healed them."

And to some extent that is Ana's inspiration. "Do something different and maybe the locals or the surroundings will not understand but other people might, and you can change a little of the vibration around and bring something to the environment because of that.

"Yoga Bled is my inspiration for everything that I do now. If you really have this enthusiastic energy and if you believe from the heart you can create this.

It has changed everything in my life. How I look at myself, how I look at others, how I go through my life. I found creative energy. It brought me growth; I could never have imagined I could go that deep. It's deep growth."

If you want to find out when the next Yoga Bled session will be held, and where it will pop up, you can get details from their Facebook page [facebook.com/yogabled] and the website is [www.yogabled.com].

Sessions normally cost €10 and includes the use of a yoga mat. You should book ahead by phone, or contact the team on Facebook and Twitter @YogaBled

Inside Knowledge
What should young people know.

"You have to hang out with the locals. Connect, talk, they will tell you where you can go to have fun, or take you to the river banks and the places we like

"In the evening we hang out in the Kult Bar very good bar, they have concerts. Our friends meet there and if you want to meet young locals that's the place to go.

"I love the Okarina festival – I would love to see more of that here.

Go to the lake you will find locals. The lake is the connector of everything.

Ana Pirih – Yoga Bled

Lea Ferjan – Bled Castle and Bled Cultural Institute

At the height of the summer more than 3,000 people visit Bled Castle each day, although it rarely feels packed or too busy. "It's so nice to meet people from all over the world there." Says Lea Ferjan. The castle is open all year and is a centre for artistic and cultural events ranging from the regular exhibitions of (usually) Slovenian artists in the gallery above the print workshop, to the medieval enactments, to playing host as one of the venues for the ethno-music Okarina Festival and classical Festival Bled. Not forgetting the traditional music, dancing, storytelling and celebration of Slovenian wine on St Martin's Day.

The 1000-year-old Bled Castle and Festival Hall are managed by Bled Cultural Institute, established in 2007. Lea Ferjan is head of marketing and sales. "Bled Castle is our beautiful heritage." She says. "It is important for Slovenia and is known around the world. It is one of the most visited sites in Slovenia. Bled Castle is in excellent condition and it is a real-life place with its printing works, wine cellar and forge that people can visit." While Bled is usually identified by the island and church, the prominent castle is a striking symbol, too, of this historic town.

There are two astonishing views from the castle. The classic view from the upper terrace is of the lake. From right to left, there are the hills Ojstrica and Mala Osojnica. As your eye moves to the left, you will see the outline of Mt. Babji Zob, below it is the hamlet Mlino and the pletna boats going to and from the island. Of course, there is the church on the island. Further to the left Straža hill, then you can see Bled centre and behind it, far out in the distance the towns, villages and steeples of the many churches in this part of Gorenjska.

"As you look down below the castle you can see the spire of St Martin's church and the swimming area called Grajsko kopališče (Castle's swimming area), which is very popular in summer season. The water is warm but refreshing. You can see the fishes in the lake from the castle terraces."

Then cross the courtyard and climb the steps to look over the walls on the northern side of the castle. Lea describes the view. "You can admire the Karavanke mountains in the distance, the national border with Austria and the Julian Alps."

When you are there, you will find other rooms to explore. "The new room there with hints of what people can see around Bled describing what is to be found in the town and the surroundings, and what to do and visit." The audio-visual display was installed less than three years ago. It tells the history of the region from ancient times, the architecture and buildings of the area, the sporting successes and much more.

"I think that most people don't take enough time to discover every part of the castle. If you wish you can be there the whole day. Not just the museum and the wine cellar and the printing works. You can enjoy being on the terrace, the morning sun, perhaps a concert in the evening or a romantic supper under the stars in the warm evening." Lea says there is a special feeling about the place "I always get a lot of energy there."

Lea grew up in Bled and like many people who make the town what it is today. She talked about life was like when she was young. "Our parents just told us when we had to be at home in the evening. The streets and gardens were our playgrounds. It was a childhood with lots of freedom and adventures of youth. We spent summer days on the lake shore, the winter weekends on ski slopes and in ice arena. It was a fantastic part of the life. It was the childhood with the limits, but not so ordered like nowadays."

Life for youngsters then and now was and is spent outdoors. "When I was a child living in Jermanka I was about 2 kilometres

from the primary school, so I got there by bicycle. It's about the same distance to work from where I live now."

Now Lea walks to work from Rečica to her office in Festivalna dvorana (Festival Hall). Most of that is a stroll around the lake. "I try to walk to my office every day and this is really my privilege because my first job was in Ljubljana. You could spend an hour and a half or two hours sitting in the car to get there. There was not a motorway from Bled to Ljubljana then." She was working in one in the computer centre of one of Yugoslavia's biggest companies, but she always wanted to work in tourism and after several tries she found a job in Bled Tourist Board in 2001.

Lea remembers when tourism in the area was less organised. Although there were hotels in the town, families would offer visitors a place to stay. "I remember that people would rent one or two rooms in their house. There were hotels in Bled, but people rented rooms and apartments and they constantly improved the standards." This still happens, and you will see many houses with a sign "Sobe" (Rooms) indicating that they take paying guests. There has been a marked rise in the number of places on Air BnB in recent years.

"Hospitality is a tradition here and if you look back over the last years the standard is better. People did well renting rooms to supplement the family budget. And I think people in Bled have a better life because of tourism."

Lea's daughter recently began attending the tourism and catering college in Bled. "My daughter decided to study tourism when she finished school for media in Radovljica. The college in the town is very important for Bled and I hope that a lot of local people will recognise that they have an opportunity to study here and to find a job in tourism. It's a hard profession because you work on national holidays, harder in summer months, but that's not a

problem if you like that work. It's a great career." Her son, a professional hockey player is as a tourist guide during the summer. "He played ice hockey abroad for many years and was also able to promote Bled. Many of his sports friends have visited him in Bled."

While the castle is a cultural and tourism centre with theatrical performances concerts on the terrace and in the Knights Hall, it is also a venue for weddings. "When I talk to the couple who are planning the wedding, I ask them how they came to decide to have the ceremony here in Bled – in the castle. They often say that the first time they came to Bled they visited the castle and decided this would be the place to get married."

Plans for 2018 include more events, but practically more work on the castle structure and amenities. "This year, 2018, is European year for cultural heritage, and it is a great opportunity for us to do even more. So, we are organising traditional events and performances in July and August, Festival Bled and Okarina Festival. Other events will be held in the town centre below the castle. The castle is in a small area and it is difficult to organise everything there." But for the events in Bled centre Bled Castle is the amazing scenery, special in the dark.

For years there has been an aspiration to build a road bypassing the town to take the traffic not bound for Bled which can cause chaos at the height of the summer. "This year we will start to renew the building on the opposite side to the museum on the upper terrace where the restaurant is and then the terraces and I think when the by-pass is completed at the end of June the Bled Cultural Institute will build new parking area under the castle. It will be near the football pitch and the George Best Back Packers' bar. at the main Castle entrance. It may be just for buses this year, and later it will be the main parking lot for Bled for cars too. We want to escape the traffic jam and people will reach the castle by walking and bike and maybe by local transfer helping Bled become a really green destination."

To keep up to date with events in Bled Castle see their website *www.blejski-grad.si/en/about-bled-castle*

Leo Ličof – Okarina Music Festival

Profile - Leo Ličof Founder and Artistic Director of The Okarina Festival

"I considered myself, even today, but back then when I was younger, to be a rare bird." Leo Ličof is founder and artistic director of the Okarina Festival which celebrates its 28th year in 2018. We met in his restaurant Okarina to look back at the festival's history and forward because even after all these years, Leo still has ambitions for the festival.

It all began appropriately enough with music, a trip to India and a restaurant specialising in vegetarian food. "I came back from India after I followed the Beatles example and had gone to Rishikesh." Rishikesh is in the foothills of the Himalayas and the place where Maharishi Mahesh Yogi trained The Beatles and others in transcendental meditation.

"I was inspired by so many bands playing good music."

Leo grew up, like others of his generation in Europe, listening to Radio Luxembourg and to the Dutch Radio Veronica. "I found myself really frustrated behind an Iron Curtain. All these bands were "non-moral" or even "prohibited". I am mad about music – I love music. I played the violin – the fiddle. However, it was impossible in Yugoslavia at that time to create anything."

In 1991, everything changed. Slovenia withdrew from Yugoslavia, communist leaders throughout Central and Eastern Europe lost power and Leo seized the opportunity for his own revolution.

The toughest thing was getting the support.

"So, the first thing I did was to create the festival." The first was held two months after independence in the grounds of the restaurant Leo owned on the shore of Lake Bled not far where the

Okarina restaurant is now. There were only two or three bands on the bill. The next year was much the same and from there it began to grow.

"But, after the first three or four years of being independent, old powers started regaining political influence. And they did not like someone trying to bring this music "to our beautiful country". "Listen to our folk music," they told me. In their opinion this was a "strange guy bringing strange tunes." So, they gave me no support; not moral, not financial. I kept on going – and fortunately, there were many people around who were open minded."

Individual contributions from supporters kept the festival going. His butcher gave him a small contribution, his baker the same and with these small amounts he could book another band, and then with some more money, book another. He was hanging on to the festival by his fingernails. "Another mayor came along, who did not want the festival at all. I was told 'You have the right to do it – but don't come to me for support'.

"Then a different mayor came who was a bit more open minded and he gave 2 or 3 thousand pounds. But it was the moral support that gave me the strength to carry on."

Since its inception, Okarina has been infused with local and national politics. But the whims of here today, gone tomorrow politicians have not dampened Leo's spirit or self-belief.

As he is talking we sip Indian tea, sweet and milky from the tea-pot. I notice in the background Joan Baez is singing Dylan's Forever Young. "I felt myself being a musical messiah. It was my duty to shake up a bit of consciousness of people in this region, to wake them up a bit.

"Then after 10 years I thought this is going nowhere ... 'Enough!' I thought."

There was once again, no support. So, there was no festival planned. "The mayor came to ask whether I would do the festival – I said no. But three weeks before the festival would have been due to start he came again pleading with me. 'I'll pay you – people are asking around.' Because after 10 years, people were beginning to think this is interesting."

Over the last eight years Zavod Za Kulturo Bled (the institute for Culture in Bled) has been financially supporting the Okarina festival and Leo especially mentions Špela Repnik, secretary of Zavod Za Kulturo, who helps to organize promotion, press conference and takes care of local transportation.

Even though one of his musical heroes, Paul McCartney visited the restaurant in 1985, his proudest moment is still the first year in the garden of the original restaurant. Hardly surprising. It was a wreck of a building which had been used as a restaurant. He and friends spent months clearing it out, cleaning it up, planting a garden where the first festival was held. They began to play music – mainly British and American – and added lots of vegetarian food to the menu. Leo ploughed all his profits back into the restaurant. Standards improved –the restaurant became more popular. The diplomatic corps from Ljubljana were visitors as embassies with representation in the city became frequent customers. He planted a garden. "It was a natural amphitheatre. I put a fountain in the middle – parachutes above the garden for shelter and decoration, candles, and huge iron charcoal heaters." And that was where they held the first Okarina festivals.

The better the restaurant became, the more work and investment he put into it – and consequently – unfairly perhaps – the rent increased. Eventually it was ridiculous demands for rent that drove Leo from the original restaurant to where we were sitting.

Today, the Okarina restaurant is at Ljubljanska cesta 8. He combines running the restaurant with being artistic director of the festival. Leo does almost everything himself. "I arrange everything from flights to t-shirts. Each band needs 30 or 40 emails forward and back." He also deals with all the contractual demands. "The band that has this requirement for staging, the band that has that needs conga drums to be supplied, this guy needs a flamenco guitar the other something else," Leo has been arranging all these years.

We finish our Masala Chai and I get ready to leave. Then in a sentence Leo encapsulated the idea of Okarina. "To create an atmosphere where people can start communicating – this is what we need most in the world, and in these mountains, even more."

For more information on the Okarina Festival, visit the website [*www.festival-okarina.si/en/*] and the Okarina restaurant is [*www.okarina.com/en/*]

The line-up for this year's festival is:

Venue: Bled Castle
25 July 8:30 pm   Dimitris Mystakidis, Greece
26 July 8:30 pm Waldemar Bastos, Angola

Venue: Promenade Bled
28 July 8:30 pm Gato Preto, Mozambique
29 July 8:30 pm Bokante, Guadalupe, USA
30 July 8:30 pm Deluxe, France
31 July 8:30 pm Los Mirlos, Peru
1 August 8:30 pm Dakh Daughters, Ukraine
2.August 8:30 pm Richard Thompson, UK
3 August 5:00 pm Yip's Children's Choir, Hong Kong and
 8:30 pm Fanfare Chokarlia, Romania
4 August 8:30 pm Guillaume Perret, France
5 August 8:30 pm Natacha Atlas, Egypt, UK

Matjaž Repnik - Diving in Lake Bled

Profile – Matjaž Repnik, Diving Instructor

Matjaž Repnik has been teaching diving at Lake Bled for about three years. He and other enthusiasts also participate in the annual lake clean up. When I spoke to him in Mlino, near the pletna pier over a few bottles of Laško, he was preparing to pack up to go home after a long day in and on the lake.

Until 2010 Matjaž was working in IT in Radovljica a town with a beautiful old centre about 15 minutes away from Bled. He swapped his desk job for diving and is now a full-time instructor working in Bled, on the Slovenia coast and Croatia. During the winter in 2016 and 2017 he worked in Sri Lanka. Matjaž has made over 1,000 dives and is in (and under) the water six times a week during the summer.

"Lake Bled has around six different diving spots. It is biologically diverse and interesting," Matjaž tells me. As we stood at the lake shore he talks about the variety of fish and fauna under the water. "There is something like eighteen different species in the lake. You will find carp, catfish, pike, zander, trout, perch and there are smaller species, too as well as the underwater plants." Almost every day of the year you will see anglers fishing from the shore, most staying awake overnight and making early morning catches. The biggest fish found in the lake was a common carp weighted 30.7 kilograms and was about 2 metres long.

The water lilies are just beginning to come alive on the surface of the water as we look out across the lake. "The visibility is pretty good at about 3 metres. We dive only to 10 metres. But the lake goes down to 30 metres where visibility is zero and temperature is only 6 degrees."

At its longest, Lake Bled is 2,120 m (6,960 ft) and widest at 1,380 m (4,530 ft). It attracts swimmers from around the world, some because of the potential healing qualities of the water. In high summer the lake temperature can reach over 21c.

"The Discover Scuba Diving course is an elementary introduction to scuba diving. I take only two people at a time. They get a taste of the excitement and the experience. They won't see everything hidden under the surface in one or two dives, but it does give novices the opportunity to taste the experience."

Divers also help keep the lake clean. "Twice in its history, Lake Bled has been close to death, almost killed off by algae." Significant steps were taken a few decades ago to ensure the health of the lake. "Last Saturday," says Matjaž, "Was Cleaning Day for the lake. Divers came from all over Slovenia. I was helping clean just where we are now in Mlino."

What did they find down there? "I couldn't bring out part of a car engine! There was an old toilet and crockery. Each diver brought out a huge bag of rubbish."

Sadly, even though there is a medieval castle and an ancient church on Lake Bled and a civilisation of over 1000 years, Matjaž has not yet found any lost treasure. About a centimetre of silt forms on the bottom of the lake every year and over time any "treasures" have either been found or covered up by nature. Or perhaps were never there at all.

Watching a film about diving changed his career path and his life. "In the village where I am from in the Culture Centre, people give photo presentations and talks about places they have been. One guy had been to Mexico and had made an underwater movie. As I watched, I saw the bubbles created by the divers breathing apparatus. I had never seen anything like that before. I was inspired by those bubbles."

The decision to be a diving instructor was made. From Slovenia, Matjaž headed to Gran Canaria to train and to work for 3 months. He moved on to Croatia where he qualified as a diving instructor. Once qualified he moved to Malaysia for seven months and worked as diving instructor. Then back to Slovenia and Austria where he now works full time and has founded his own diving club.

"I am a PADI instructor and a course here in Bled or in Slovenia is recognised anywhere in the world. The Discover Scuba Diving course is a onetime event, but if someone wants to do something more advanced I can do that with them. Next level is an Open Water Course. You can come here and do that in three or four days. There are dives and skills and safety training. And I teach you to navigate under water with a compass. After that you can dive up to 18 metres anywhere in the world. If you are already a diver and are looking for a dive buddy, if you bring your certification we can dive together.

"Today I was running a Rescue Course and some tourists from the Netherlands stopped when they saw the equi pment and they wanted to know about diving in Lake Bled. I explained the way I am explaining to you. So now I am going to be organising a dive for them."

For more information or make a booking you can contact Matjaž via his website watersports.si/en/contact Or email him ahead of your visit to Slovenia at info@watersports.si

Bled - Insider Knowledge:

I like the walk on little hill called Dobra Gora altitude 625m . From where I live I walk in the direction of direction Dinol (part of the town) south east. It is about 1h to walk from my house. The climb takes about 25-30 min. It is pretty steep but on top is stunning view on Jelovice area and Ribno village. It is never crowded with people. Even locals don't go to much.

Luka of Hotel Garni Berc

Voted Tripadvisor's "Best Hotel in Bled" many years in succession.

PART 6 – STORIES AND IDEAS

What should I not miss on my first visit?

It's a simple question with so many possible answers. "Do you have any tips when I visit Bled?"

It's easier if I know you and what you like to do, what time of the year you are going, who you will be with. But in general, these are my top tips.

1- Do you like pubs?
Depending on your taste in pubs, Pri Planincu or George Best are two of the more popular. But don't forget to try Kult in the main shopping centre, especially if you are younger.

2 - Do you like cakes?
Bled Cream Cake is famous. It was first made in the Park Hotel - try it on the terrace overlooking the lake. My own favourite patisserie is Slascicarna Zima where there is a massive selection of cakes.

3 - Do you like history and castles?
Then you must go to Bled Castle. It's easy to spend the best part of a day there, especially when the theatrical groups are performing medieval stories.

4 - Do you like Yoga?
Contact the lovely people at Bled Yoga details here: yogabled.com/

5 - Do you like pizza?
Pri Planincu or Pizzeria Rustika - there are others, but I've not tried them all.

6- Do you like music?
Then the Okarina Festival for Ethno/World music, Festival

Bled for classical music. Check out events in the Festival Hall and Bled

Castle There is live music during the summer at Park Hotel Terrace. There is traditional Slovenian music in some other hotels occasionally. If you are there in the winter don't miss Folk Music Hit Parade 2018.

7 - Do you like to walk?
Obviously walk around the lake – it takes about 90 minutes. There are lots of easy walks and a few more testing ones. Best to ask advice or talk to a local and get them to tell you their favourite places. If you like a good long walk, why not try escaping to some of the other nearby villages like Vrba or walk all the way to Vintgar and then the gorge.

8 - Do you like swimming?
During the summer, the best times to swim in the lake are early in the morning or in the evening to cool off. There are even organised winter swimming events if you are hardcore.

9 - Do you like hiking?
Try the hills around Bled and of course Vintgar Gorge.

10 Do you like to sit on a warm evening just enjoying the vibe?
Try Vila Prešeren.

11 Do you like custom made jewellery?
Visit Široka Huberto opposite the Toplice Hotel.

12 - Do you like horses and horse drawn carriages?
The fijaker stand is beside the Festival Hall?

13- Do you like wine?
Visit Vinoteka Zdravljica to sample some of the best and most affordable Slovenian wines.

14 - Do you like Indian food?
Try Okarina. You know, the place Paul McCartney liked so much.

15 - Will you be there at Christmas?

Make a point of going to St Martin's Church (the beautiful white church at the beginning of a path to the Castle) for Mass on Christmas Eve. The nativity scene is beautiful and on the busiest of days you will find real tranquillity.

The Antimuseum

Ljubljanska cesta, 27, Bled, Slovenia
Phone+386 30 346 364

Most people heading to Bled are expecting beautiful scenery, warm weather, fine food. One thing you really should not miss if you have children is the Antimuseum.

It is only one room in the building that houses Infocenter Triglavska roža Bled and permanent Triglav exhibition, but it s filled with exciting physics experiments. It is a place intended to fire the imagination (child or not). Objects levitate, lightening is created, a plasma gun fires flashes and bangs.

You could easily spend an afternoon there with the hands-on experiments.

You must book ahead. Programs begin at 12:00 on weekends, but you can call to book another time.

You will be able to hear a podcast episode featuring the Antimuseum soon.

Other things to try:

- Rent a bike.
- Rent a rowing boat.
- Visit the island.
- Take a photo from Bled Castle - use the free wifi to add it to your social media feed.
- Take a trip on pletna.
- In winter there is skiing and skating and in December a winter market.

- Try real Slovenian food.
- Burek - cheese or apple or minced meat in flaky pastry
- Ćevapčići - a little like British sausages (I did say "a little").
- kranjska klobasa - Carniolan sausage.
- Ričet - thick soup with pot barley, beans, potatoes, carrots, parsley, celery, leeks, tomatoes, onions, and garlic.

The Historic Pletna Boats

One of the great attractions for almost every visitor to Bled is the short voyage to and from the island on a pletna boat. They are unique to Bled. Why are they here at all?

Standing on the stern of the pletna, the skipper – "pletnar" – rows his 20 passengers to Bled Island. The passengers, protected from the sun (or the rain) by the colourful awning, sit low enough to dip their fingers in the lake. The pletna and enduring symbols of the area. The pletnar you see is likely to have built or helped build his flat-bottomed boat. And he – they are all men – is part of a family tradition going back almost 1000 years.

The story of the pletna boat is believed to start about 1150. The land around the hamlet Mlino on the southern coast of Lake Bled was not good enough to farm. So, families were given permission from the local authorities to ferry pilgrims to the island. It was a way to make a living, but also an effective way for the authorities to raise taxes.

In the reign of Empress Maria Theresa (who ruled from 1740 to 1780), twenty-two families were given exclusive rights to transport pilgrims to the island. Three centuries later, descendants of those families are still the exclusive operators of the pletna boats.

Pletna Today

According to skipper Marjan Zupan, the distinctive style of the modern day pletna was decided in the early 20th century. He writes about it on his website [*pletnaboat.com*] "Significant changes in building a pletna boat came in the year 1902 when it got the shape it has today. The most credit for that goes to my grandfather Anton Zupan who was involved at the construction of the pletna boat." The vessel measures 7 metres by 2 metres transports up to 20 passengers.

A young pletnar and neighbour Alex rowed my wife and me to the island as a special treat. He, his brother and father all row pletna in this family tradition. "Is it not harder work rowing 20 people rather than 2?" With more people in the boat, he tells me, the lower it sits in the water – that is what it is designed for – so filled to capacity it is easier to push through the water.

There are some old black and white photos of pletna boats and of old Bled on the exterior wall of the fire station in Mlino.

The legends of the Sunken Bell and the Wishing Bell

This story about a special bell – one that cannot be seen, but sometimes is heard. The legend tells us that it lies somewhere under the waves, near the island.

Around the year 1500 a bell had been commissioned by the wife of the Master of the castle after he had gone missing, presumed dead. When she heard about his disappearance, Hartman Kreigh's wife Poliksena was so distraught that she gathered all the gold and silver in the castle collection to pay for a new bell for the island church so that he would be remembered every time it rang. As much as his wife loved him, Kreigh was mourned by few others. Farmers had complained about him trampling on their rights and humiliating them. He was reviled by the people of Bled, Mlino and the other villages over which he had charge. Some

138

people even thought that his "disappearance" might have been at the hands of the enemies he had made in the rural community.

At his wife's command, the bell was cast. As it was being transported to the island, the weather changed dramatically. Winds became so strong that the waves of the normally calm lake crashed over the boat, fast filling it with water. The crew could not bail out quickly enough. The boat became unstable and the bell fell into the water sinking into the lake bed's mud never to be seen again. Perhaps it was a weakness in the boat's structure, perhaps it was the weight of the mighty new bell, but no one survived to tell the story. It appears that even nature had her final revenge on the loathed Kreigh.

Today, some say the bell can be heard ringing from the depths of Lake Bled.

Each Christmas evening, once the sun has gone down and darkness has come, the legend of the Sunken Bell is celebrated in a show of fire and lights, music and dance. It is among the more spectacular events of the year. Then slowly, as if by magic, the illuminated bell rises from the depths of the lake.

The Wishing Bell

After the widow Kreigh died, the Pope consecrated a new bell and sent it to the Bled Island. It is said that whoever rings this bell - the bell you can hear ring every day many times - thereby gives honour to Virgin Mary gets his wish come true.

It is a tradition to ring the bell your wish will come true.

Bled Island – its history and traditions

People have lived in this area since the Mesolithic times (5,000 to 10,000 BC). It is not difficult to imagine that even then the lake with the unique island was regarded as a spiritual place. In pre-Christian times, it was a place of pilgrimage and sacrifice. People have been visiting the island to worship right up to the present day. Although there are more tourists than pilgrims today.

There is evidence of settlements in the area from stone age, iron age and Roman times. Graves from around 600 BC have been found. The pre-Christian era ended in the 7th century. For some time, the island had been the place of worship to the goddess Živa. With the Slavic settlement, around 600 AD, and the conversion from pagan to Christian, worship of Živa was replaced by devotion to the Virgin Mary. Parts of the present-day church link back to the 15th century.

Today, occasionally, weddings are held in the church and occasionally Masses are celebrated. There is an annual Christmas concert by the wives and mothers of the Pletnars.

The entrance to the Church and Bell Tower is Adults €6.00, Students €4.00, Children €1.00 and Family ticket €12.00. People rent boats to visit the island and even swim. Getting to the island by Pletna is the traditional journey.

A pletna trip is €14 per person (€7 for children). You will be able to stay 40 minutes. Whether you think that is long enough to visit the island and appreciate the spiritual nature of the place is up to you. I find it all a bit of a rush. If you want to spend some time exploring the very beautiful church, taking time in the bell tower, the restaurant and walking around the island. In my view you need to take a lot longer. Speak to the pletnar before you go to the island. Most speak English well enough to negotiate extra time on the island.

There are five locations around the lake where you can board a pletna. They are not always staffed. The most popular places are on the boardwalks behind Hotel Park and beside Hotel Prešeren. The pier at Mlino is normally used for organised trips although you can sometimes get on board there. There is also a departure point in Velika Zaka near the camping ground, but it is not available year-round.

as mentioned, it is possible to hire a rowing boat to get to the island. Places to dock are limited. Take advice when you are renting.

There is more information on the Bled Island website [www.blejskiotok.si] Email: info@blejskiotok.si. Phone: +386 4576 79 79

Seven things to do before 7:00 am

Venture out before early breakfast and around the lake you will see photographers, people fishing, power walkers and the first pletna taking staff to the island. Are you ready to start your day good and early? These are only 7 things you can do around Lake Bled, breakfast not included.

1.   The Bells. The Bells.

Make your way to the boardwalk near the main camping site a little before 7:00 any morning. It is probably about a 40-minute walk from the town centre, almost half way around the lake. There won't be many people about. It is not silent – the air is filled with birdsong, there is the occasional quack, the odd cyclist and a runner or two.

From there you can see the island, the castle and St. Martin's church. During the summer months, you will also enjoy the sunrise. Then a few seconds before 7:00 am, a bell tolls, then another, and the sounds build. Some of the peals are from the Church of the Assumption on the island, others from St. Martin's, but there are other, more remote bells ringing, too

They all welcome a new day and peal for about four minutes. Good morning Bled.

2.   Biking, running, walking - just because it's fun

This is by far the best time to put on your trainers and get the best from running, walking and cycling around the lake, and even further. Later in the day the cyclists tangle with walkers on the paths. The runners will face walkers coming in the opposite direction. But now, there are so few people around the lakeside is all yours. The round lake route is a good 90-minute walk or 25-minute bike ride, but why not go further?

3. Sunrise Lake Bled

You don't have to be active and energetic to enjoy the morning. Just find a bench and enjoy the air, the sounds and the clear light. The south west part of the lake is the best spot for watching the sun come up behind the hills. When and where is the best sunrise? See next.

4. See the pink cloud factory at work

In the autumn, something magical happens. As the sun emerges from behind the hills, it warms the lake and the mist rises. The sun shines through the mist turning it from white to gold to yellow to pink. This is the time to take some amazing photos of the colourful mist swirling around the lake and up into the air towards the castle. It is a stunning sight. Best place to view it is probably at Zaka near the camp site.

5. Swim

There is no better way to start a summer's day in Bled than a swim in the lake. The water is warm and deep and there are many secluded corners for the shy swimmer to strike out into what many believe are healing waters. Healing or not, you will feel so much better after floating on your back watching the whips of clouds drift by above you.

6. A barefoot walk

During the summer, there is an organised barefoot walk and you can join a group of people enjoying the dew between their toes. There is no need to wait for an organised walk. Enjoy the open fields and pastures alone or with your own group of friends.

People have come to Bled for generations to enjoy the health-giving properties of the region; the water, the air and even the soft cool grass on a warm summer morning.

The 20th Rikli's Walk to Straža hill will be at 7:00 am on 1 July 2018 meeting in front of Hotel Golf.

7.   Feed the ducks?

Do not feed bread to the ducks and swans. We have all done it and the ducks seem to like it, but experts in duckie-culture advise us to vary what we give them and select healthier more natural treats like oats, corn, or defrosted frozen peas. And exercise portion control.

It is a wonderful sight to watch the ducks fly in from the other side of the lake, and scoot over the water as they land and all for some free food. If you are in one of the wider open grassy spots like Mlino in the early morning, you will see ducks and swans on the bank tugging at the grass and feeding themselves and preening in the early sun rays.

10 "Must Dos" in Bled and around Lake Bled

Most of the ideas here are not new or original. If you spend a week in Bled, you will probably do most of them without thinking about it. But if you are off the train and heading next to Ljubljana, Croatia or somewhere else and you only have a short time, here are 10 top activities to try to give you a real taste of Bled.

1.   Head for the Information Centres

There are two Information Centres in Bled; one in the main shopping area near the Casino which you should make your priority, the other is Bled Tourism Office Infocenter Triglavska roža Bled, Ljubljanska cesta 27, 4260 Bled Phone: +386 (0)4 5780 205 e-mail: info@dzt.bled.si

You should go to both if you have time. They will bring you right up-to-date with what's going on in town and around the lake. If you are a serious hiker, outdoor sports fan, or planning a visit to the Triglav National Park, then the Infocenter Triglavska roža Bled is a must for information, maps, books and advice.

2.   Go Around Lake Bled At Least Once

The top modes of transport are:

Feet and legs – walking is easily the best way to get around the lake and to explore some of the places you'll miss by going at speed. Allow 90 minutes to 2 hours. But you can really extend it if you want to. There are many coffee and snack places to re-fuel or just sit and watch the day go by.

Tourist Train – It costs €5 and takes around 25 minutes. You can hop on and hop off only once. There are stops including at Mlino, Zaka (near the large camping site), beside the boat club, near St. Martin's church and three of four places to climb aboard in town. The train departs about every 45 minutes. Check the time tables at the stops.

Bicycle – Hire a bike if you want to cover a lot of ground independently. A quick once around the lake takes 30 – 45 minutes. But try to avoid busy times of the day. Cyclists are not greater beings than other visitors, they have no priority, even though some think they do. It is astonishing how rude many cyclists are to walkers. The trip is not all flat, but it is not a challenging ride. There is information about bike hire elsewhere in this book.

Horse drawn carriage – This is going to cost €50, but up to 4 people can travel together. The journey takes about 25 to 30 minutes. You will find the coachmen (fijaker) beside Festival Hall. They will take you to other destinations including the castle. There is a list of destinations and prices.

3. Visit the Island

It is an experience. Some people do it every visit, for others once is enough. The most common ways to get there are:

By Pletna – These are the flat-bottomed boats. The return fare is €14. There are piers at 5 points around the lake. It is a lovely trip, however once you reach the island, might want more than 40 minutes there. Talk to your Pletnar before departing to find out if you may return in a different boat. (The Pletnar is the pletna captain.)

Rent a boat and row which will cost from around €12 per hour. The advantage with rowing is that you decide timings, and there is a place to tie up on the island. The disadvantage is ... well you have to row. Take advice when you are hiring about rules for docking at the island.

Hydrobus leaves from the pier behind the Park Hotel Terrace on the hour 10:00, 11:00, 12:00, 14:00, 15:00, 16:00, 17:00, 18:00. Adults pay €11, children €6. You should talk to the operator about how long you can stay on the island.

You could swim, but if you want to go into the Church you'll need to wear more than Speedos.

Why go? Lots of reasons -

- Climb the 100 steps - or get someone to carry you.
- Visit the church - ancient and graceful.
- Climb the clock tower.
- Ring the Wishing Bell.
- Different views across the lake.
- Find a quiet corner and think or meditate.
- Visit an exhibition.
- Get the T-Shirt (literally). There is a shop on the island with some very nice collectables.

4. Eat Lunch

You can go from 5-star grandeur at the more expensive hotels to a tuna roll from Mercator sitting on a bench beside the lake.

My tip – Burek from Pekarna Planika (Triglavska cesta 43, 4260 Bled). This is a fantastic little bakery open from 6:00 am. Burek is a term than encompasses a range of traditional food. In this case, it is crumbly pastry with various fillings such as potato and onion (krompir), cheese (sir), or mixed meats and for desert, apple. You will find it on the road from the bus station going towards town.

There is an extensive list of other places to eat in this book including many personal recommendations.

5. Eat Cake

OK, it is easy to become controversial here. Bled cream cake is what everyone talks about. It is part of the marketing of the town – part of the marketing of Slovenia. Fair enough. You can get it almost anywhere – Park Hotel's Terrace has the history and the setting – but up past the bus station toward the castle is Slaščičarna Zima – possible the best pastry shop on the planet. They have Bled cream cake, too, but so much more.

The only way to know which is better is to try both; one in the morning the other in the afternoon. Other providers of Bled cream cake are available, everywhere.

6. Head for higher ground

One of the first thing you will notice about Bled is that it is surrounded by hills. Each has a different stunning view of the lake.

Straža and castle hills are both fairly accessible. Straža even has a chair lift to get you up and summer tobogganing to get you down. Summer tobogganing is excellent fun and should be separate on this list, but there is so much to fit in.

To get to castle, you can climb a few hundred steps up the side of the hill if you are fit enough. Starting from the steps at St Martin's Church is probably easiest. You could walk from the bus station past the George Best Bar and up along the road. At times during the summer season, there is a bus. A taxi which will probably cost about €10 from the town centre. Entrance to the castle is €9.

If you are fit enough and are prepared for a challenge you could try Ojstrica and Mala Osojnica the hills where some of the most famous photos of Lake Bled are taken. But it can be tough going if you have spent your working life behind a desk.

Ojstrica rises to 611 metres and the Mala Osojnica viewpoint is at 670 metres. Coming down from Mala Osojnica towards the lake can be difficult. If you are unsure, get advice.

Another view is from the Bled Jezero train station. Nice view - not terribly high, though. But there is a bar ...

7. Go Somewhere Else

If you are staying in Bled for more than a day, then Vintgar Gorge is a must. It's not too far to walk to, but there is a bus during the summer.

The Hop On - Hop Off bus will take you to nearby villages and towns (if it is operating when you are there). Or you could use Bled as a base and turn to the next chapter for suggestions of other places to visit.

There are many marked and signposted walks. As you follow the paths you will see signs encouragingly pointing you in the right direction. You can find routes in "Bled – City Map" and "Bled – A Tourist Map" which you can get from Tourist Information and other tourism outlets.

There are guided tours including walking tours around the lake where an expert will point out things you might miss otherwise.

8. Swim

Well, it's a lake, people have been coming for the water here for almost 200 years.

There are lots of swimming places around Lake Bled. There are lots of fishing places too, so be considerate. Where's best? The Public Lido is best if you like to have a place to store your clothes and there is a busy bar and restaurant adjacent. Mlino attracts sunbathers and swimmers but getting in and out of the water is not quite so easy there. There are steps to ease yourself in just on the right as you look to the castle from the coffee shack. Zaka Camping also attracts sunbathers and families too. There is a pier to jump off, but it is easy just to walk into the water.

And the water itself? In the summer the water can get up to 30c I have been told (although I find it hard to believe). That might be an exaggeration but is comfortably warm at the height of the season. And there are people who swim in clubs during the coldest days of winter.

Best time in spring and summer for a quiet swim is always in the morning or in the evening when the crowds have gone. But even if you don't swim you can sit at the edge of the lake and dip your toes.

9. St. Martin's Church

The church of the Assumption of Mary on the Island rightly gets a lot of attention. Whether you are a church goer or not, the parish church St. Martin's is a cool and shaded escape on a hot sunny day, or a place for quiet contemplation all year. Over Christmas there is a beautiful nativity scene.

In this region of Slovenia, there is no shortage of churches – big and small, by the road or high in the hills. There may be as many as 3,000 in the country. St. Martin's was built between 1903 to 1905. Among the beautiful frescos is one portraying Vladimir Lenin as Judas Iscariot in a depiction of the Last Supper. Do remember, this is a church where the faithful come to worship, not just on Sunday. So, please be respectful.

10. Start planning your return

This happens more often than you might expect, not for everyone, but half way through a visit, some people realise that there is more to see, do and experience than they had expected. For us it was "I wonder what the lake is like in the winter." If you are one of the many who are captivated, now is the time to think about what you are going to do on your return.

And book early. Once Easter passes, accommodation becomes more difficult to find for the summer. Bled is a 12-month destination, so other times of the year are easier – and less expensive – to book.

PART 7 –
BLED AS A BASE

Usually, people make Ljubljana a base and take trips from there. Bled can also be a starting point for the whole of the Gorenjska region. There is not enough room here for an exhaustive list of all the places you can go, but here are a few ideas.

Insider knowledge - Triglav National Park

You could spend weeks in Triglav – a lifetime exploring. Tomaz Piber's has lived in Bled all his life, and the Piber family, for generations. His suggestion for his insider secret to Bled, takes us right out of the town and into the heart of the national park.

"If you are making a short visit, one place you could focus on is Pocar Homestead, a museum decorated house, considered one of the oldest homesteads in the park. You will find a rich collection, themed on life in the towns near Triglav over the centuries. During the summer months, the barn homestead event space is used for cultural and creative presentations."

Pocar Homestead is in Mojstrana, 30-minute drive from Bled or by bus via Lesce on the way to Kranjska Gora.

Open on Saturdays and Sundays and holidays from 11:00 am to 6:00 pm. Zgornja Radovna 25, SI-4281 Mojstrana. Phone 386 (0) 4 578 0200, 386 (0) 4 578 02

For more information and more detail on opening hours, check [www.kranjska-gora.si/en/sightseeing/cultural-sights/homesteads-and-houses/pocar-homestead] or call

Kranjska Gora tourist information 386 4 580 94 40 e-mail: info@kranjska-gora.eu

Go to Italy for lunch

One of the most beautiful day trips from Bled is by train to Nova Gorica on the border with Italy. Not only are Nova Gorica (Slovenia) and Gorizia (Italy) attractive places to visit, the train journey itself is an experience.

The route begins at Jesenice railway station, but you can join the train at Bled Jezero. The journey takes you through the historic Bohinj railway route. Following the Soča River most of the way, the train travels over high bridges, viaducts and through tunnels up to 6,000 metres long.

As you pass over the Solkan Bridge, you might not notice much except you are so high and there is a fabulous view. The view of the bridge, which you won't see from the train, is something special, too. Search the web for photos. Solkan Bridge is an astonishing and beautiful fete of engineering.

The 219.7 metre bridge over the Soča River is near Nova Gorica. With an arch span of 85 metres (279 ft), it was originally built between 1900 and 1905, and officially opened in 1906.

In the same year, the Bohinj Tunnel, which connected central Europe with Trieste, was opened by the heir presumptive to the Austro-Hungarian throne, Franz Ferdinand. At Bohinj station there is a small exhibition about the tunnel and the historic railway construction.

Nova Gorica and Gorizia

The train station is only a few metres from the Italian border and when you arrive you can choose which town to visit; the modern Yugoslavian/Slovenian Nova Gorica (a 20-minute walk) or the old Italian town Gorizia (a 30 minute walk).

"In 1947, following World War II, Italy signed a peace treaty with the Allies, including Socialist Yugoslavia. The treaty transferred most of the Slovenian-inhabited

areas of the Italian Province of Gorizia to Yugoslavia. The town of Gorizia, itself, however, remained under Italian rule. The new border was drawn in a way that cut the city off its north-eastern surroundings and left around 40% of the territory of the municipality to Yugoslavia, including the suburbs of Solkan, Šempeter, Kromberk, Rožna Dolina, and Pristava. The Communist authorities of the Socialist Republic of Slovenia therefore decided to build a new settlement in the area just along the new border, linking the former suburbs of Gorizia into a new urban space, named Nova Gorica or New Gorizia. The first projects were laid out in late 1947, and the construction began at the beginning of the following year.

Wikipedia [https://en.wikipedia.org/wiki/Nova_Gorica]

Once you have inspected the Italian Slovenian frontier follow the road south (or turn left out of the station). You will be walking parallel with the border. At the T-junction turn right for Italy and left for Nova Gorica. Walk around, follow your nose – try to find the main square in Gorizia and if you want a stand-by recommendation for somewhere to have lunch, I've been to Pizzeria Al Lampione - Via Silvio Pellico 7 Gorizia, twice and enjoyed it both times.

You can go any day by the ordinary train service from Jesenice – which stops at Jezero Bled and takes a little under 2 hours. There is enough time to walk to either town for lunch. If you are planning a longer visit, check the timetables on the Slovenian Railways website.

The normal fare is €6.59 (Children aged 6 to 12, €3.30. The young persons' fare for people aged 12 to 26 is €4.61. You can also get a weekend return. Tourist return trip on weekends and public

holidays is a fantastic deal €9.22 (prices correct as of 1 March 2018). Please check the Slovenian Railways website for any changes (but those prices have remained stable for at least 3 years).

The Heritage Train

As an alternative to scheduled journey, you can transport yourself back in time 100+ years and try the Heritage Train package with departures in 2018 from Jesenice and Bled Jezero in May (5th, 12th, 19th), June (2nd, 9th, 16th, 23rd, 30th), July (7th ,21st), August (11th , 18th), September (8th, 15th 22nd, 29th) October (6th, 13th, 27th), and 3rd November. The price is €41 adults with children's' concessions.

These stream-train trips are very popular and sell out early. Don't expect to turn up and buy a ticket. Advance seat reservations are required.

You will be accompanied by actors dressed in period costume including a couple portraying Franz Joseph and his wife.

More on the Slovenian Railway website. [*www.slo-zeleznice.si/en/passenger-transport/around-slovenia/heritage-trains/take-the-heritage-train-along-the-bohinj-line*]

An easy morning and lunch in Radovljica

Radovljica. The name looks like a mouthful. But really, it's not. Try "Radol'ca".

To get there take a short bus journey or even an off-road cycle ride. After the bus stops at Lesce, the Radovljica bus station is next. The old town is just past the DM chemist shop and across the car park. It is always busy around the bus station; anyone will point you in the right direction.

Why are we going there? First to look at the beautiful old buildings. Many have been renovated over the last few years restoring them to how they must have looked in the 15th and 16th century when they were built. The main street in the old town is short but manages to squeeze in two museums, two restaurants, a café, shops, a church and accommodation, and more.

If you have a sweet tooth, then this is the place for you. Honey, honey bread, ginger bread and chocolate. If you have a sweet tooth then you will need to know that each April there is a festival of chocolate, the largest offering of chocolate, chocolate dishes and chocolate desserts in all of Slovenia.

Gingerbread Museum and Workshop

In the basement of Gostilna Lectar, there is an authentic workshop where the famous gingerbread hearts are made. Gingerbread hearts are not unique to Radovljica or even Slovenia, but here you can watch them being made and even (if you ask nicely) help in the process. It is great for adults – and tremendous for children. You can also buy honey bread.

The first gingerbread bakery was established here in 1766. In 1822, the owners opened the restaurant. In 2006, they renovated and opened the vaulted rooms as a working bakery. For more details and opening hours check the website [*www.lectar.com*].

The restaurant is very traditional, and the food is excellent – my favourite is mushroom soup in a bowl of hollowed out bread.

Another excellent restaurant for lunch looking out over the hills behind the town is Gostilna Avguštin, Linhartov trg 15, 4240 Radovljica.

The first time I visited Bled in 1996, a friend told me there was a beekeeping museum in Radovljica, I had no idea how important apiculture is in Slovenia and this region. There is a map in the museum showing that bees from the surrounding countryside have been exported to the world. In nearby Lesce there is the Gorenjska Region Beekeeping Development and Education Centre. In a world where bees are reportedly on the decrease, apiculture is a serious business. It is also an historic and colourful business. There is a wonderful display of all sorts of beehives and decorative panels collected over the centuries. The historic panels capture the history and the culture of the region. They show scenes of family life (not always "PC"), religion, superstitions and fears. There are beehives like intricate dolls houses. One is a wooden man at least 3 metres high. Modern hives have brightly coloured panels.

There is a wonderful antique or curiosity shop where you can spend a lot of time digging through a mass of early 20th century technology including radios, furniture, WWII medals, musical instruments, and folk art.

The Tourist Office can provide information and suggestions of even more places to see around this beautiful area. It is right at the top of the old town. Ask about the free sightseeing tour of Radovljica's Old Town which usually happens every Tuesday at 10.00 am. It I organised by Radovljica Tourist Information Centre.

For more information about Radovljica, the events and the Chocolate Festival, the website is [*www.radolca.si/en*]

Kranjska Gora

This is almost a perfect day trip for anyone including families. You can get to Kranjska Gora by bus (change at Lesce. Check timetables – I find a Google search is best). The bus journey can take up to two hours to get there.

Insider Knowledge: Annoyingly, the bus from Bled to Lesce arrives within one minute or less of the bus from Lesce to Kranjska Gora. If there is any hold up, you can end up waiting for the next bus – 30 or 40 minutes depending on the time of day.

If you can drive it will only take about half an hour by the highway. All the better having a car. It means you can tour around the area and visit places like the famous Russian Chapel which was built in 1917 by Russian prisoners of war in memory of the deceased during the construction of the Vršič Pass road. If you enjoy driving twisting hairpin corners the road up to the Pass and down again to Bovec. It takes around an hour, but you should stop from time to time to enjoy the view and the air.

In winter Kranjska Gora is a centre for snow sport activity, predominantly skiing. And in the summer, there are plenty of outdoor activities. This is a centre for cycling and hiking. For children (and adults) there is summer sledding, roller skating and Fairy-tale Land. These are just a few examples. There are extensive winter and summer activities for all ages and levels of fitness.

If you just want to mooch about and take it easy, there is a very pretty – and very small - Alpine old town. Restaurants and coffee shops galore. The bright yellow Restaurant and Pizzeria Kotnik is a favourite. Café London at the Ramada hotel has an excellent apple strudel. An organised culinary journey once a week, visits five eateries. Find out about that at the tourist information office.

If you are driving, with a bit of research you can plan your own tour. Although I am yet to try it, there is a glass topped tour bus giving 360-degree views. It connects places and attractions in the Upper Sava Valley.

The Tourist Information Centre in the town is at Kolodvorska ul. 1c 4280 Kranjska Gora Phone: +386 (0)4 580 94 40 e-mail: info@kranjska-gora.eu

The new website is very useful to help pick out the highlights [*www.kranjska-gora.si/en*]

Kranj, Škofja Loka and Tržič

In many ways, Kranj is an ordinary, busy small city, but there are several things to look out for on a visit. Start with Prešeren's House and Prešeren Grove. Prešeren is Slovenia's national poet. There are links to him in Bled, but this is where he lived and practiced.

See the Kokra River canyon just below the town and the bridges crossing it. There's the very beautiful and strange Plečnik's arcade and fountain. Near the **Prešeren** Museum you'll find Janez Puhar's house; Puhar was the inventor of glass photography. There is a labyrinth of tunnels under the town. For access to those as part of a guided tour contact Tourist Information: Glavni trg 2, 4000 Kranj Phone: +386 (0)4 238 04 50 e-mail: info@tourism-kranj.si

Other places to visit and spend time in include the beautiful **Škofja Loka** [*www.visitskofjaloka.si/en*] with its old town, castle and grand houses and countryside to explore.

The small but intriguing **Tržič;** wander through its entries and pathways and find the museum which tells the story of shoe making in the region. Believe me, it is a lot more interesting than that sentence would suggest. Tržiški muzej, 4290 Tržič, Phone: +386 4 592 38 10.

If you are going by bus, there are two routes from Bled to **Tržič**. The route via Begunje na Gorenjskem and Slatna has great views south. Journey time is about 30 minutes by car, an hour by bus from Bled station.

Some people try to compare Bled and **Bohinj** claiming one is better than another. It is neither a wise not fair comparison. Someone might prefer one over the other (many people in Bled head to Bohinj every chance they get), but that is as far as a comparison can go. They are different places with different offerings. Bohinj, was among the 20 shortlisted destinations competing for the title of the Best European Destination of 2018.

Some activities are similar. I always think (right or wrong) that Bohinj is for the outdoor active person and Bled is mainly for the outdoor leisurely type. Why don't you do the comparison yourself? Bohinj is just about half an hour away by bus (Bohinj Jezero or Bohinj Zlatorog). The train goes to Bohinjska Bistrica (about an hour's walk to the lake in beautiful countryside).

Begunje na Gorenjskem is a favourite with an excellent restaurant and the Slavko Avsenik Museum. If you want to start collecting traditional Gorenjska costume or get a highly decorated and polished accordion, this is the place to visit.

Kropa might not be on your list of places to visit, but really should make the effort, particularly if you like decorative iron work (in which the town abounds) and social history that makes you glad you are living in the 21st century. Try to take the bus that offers you the free walking tour - although the visit to the museum will cost about €3. Kropa is in the Hop On Hop Off bus route.

Insider knowledge - Ljubljana

Many people who come to Bled are visiting Ljubljana or basing themselves there. Visit Ljubljana has a marvellous website which has all the information you need for a visit. As there is so much to choose from let me provide one "insider tip". During the summer visit Ljubljana on a Friday for the Open Kitchen (Odprta kuhna). Ljubljana has many attractions. This is one of the best. Locals, tourists, office workers, passers-by enjoy the food from around the country and around the world, cooked in open-air kitchens for a fraction of the cost of a formal restaurant. And chefs and restaurateurs from Slovenia and beyond show off their best food. Dependent on weather.

Christmas Market in Villach

This may be a tad over imaginative, but I see the small train station at Lesce, known as Lesce-Bled, as the first step to anywhere in Europe. Or beyond, come to that. Several times a day the train to Ljubljana stops. The usual commuter train passes Kranj and Škofja Loka arriving in Ljubljana after about an hour. It's faster than the bus, but if you are staying in Bled, you still must make the connection between there and Lesce and Bled. During the day, there is a frequent bus service which is patchier in the evenings.

From Ljubljana, you can travel on, south to Belgrade (for as little as €29) and on from there – Istanbul is only a 24-hour train ride. East from Ljubljana, there are parts of Slovenia to explore; Celje, Maribor, Ptuj, Murska Sobota (I recommend them all) or across the border into Hungary and on to Budapest.

Going north, twice a day, a train to Munich (5 and a half hours) or Salzburg (4 hours).

Maybe you don't have all the time in the world.

If you are in Bled at Christmas, once you have checked out the town's Winter Fairytale, take the train from Lesce to another market, this time the Advent market in Villach, the first main town across the border in Austria.

I like to explore, sometimes just turn up in town and see what's happening. The first time I to Villach, I didn't know there was an Advent market here. I just took a train ride and a chance to explore a new town.

Car or Train?

There is little difference between the time it takes by car (about 45 minutes) and the train journey (about 50 minutes), but you will need the proper documents if you drive. The information on what you need is at the end of this chapter.

If you take the train, just step on and I suggest on the way north you sit on the right. You will have the best views there.

Jesenice is the last stop before leaving Slovenia. It's an industrial city but you will see some spectacular scenery from the train. Slovenia and Austria are separated by the Karawanks, (or Karavankas or Karavanks), a limestone mountain range under which runs the Karawanks Tunnel where somewhere along the 5-mile stretch, Slovenia meets Austria and you emerge on the other side with a different mobile phone service and some – but not may – clues that you are in a different country.

Faaker See

The train passes above Lake Faak (in German, Faaker See and in Slovenian, Baško jezero). This is a beautiful lake (one for "the bucket list"). A little bigger than Bled, turquoise water, boats and yachts and on the Drava. Bled is on the Sava. There is a train station here if you are tempted – maybe one for the summer, though.

Villach Train Station

I like to arrive and explore. Sometimes I find nothing. Sometimes after twenty minutes, I realise I'm going entirely the wrong direction and heading out of town. Sometimes there is a small adventure, a story or just a good lunch waiting to be found. Villach was all three. Without really planning anything or thinking about where I was going, I walked to the street opposite the main train station, Bahnhofstrasse and kept on going. It was a lovely walk – mid December, sunshine, cold, but a welcoming cold, past a beautiful church at Nikolaiplatz and on down to the river Drava over Villach Draubrücke. The bridge bedecked with flags from (all?) the countries in the European Union. It has been a traditionally strategic crossing point for centuries. The embankments along the river are now built up and are used by walkers and cyclists. This is a region where cycling is popular.

Over the Bridge

Once across the bridge, you enter the old town. There is a lot more to explore in a couple of hours than I managed. There is no traffic, this has been a pedestrianised area for years. You can really begin to appreciate the buildings and the layout. And as always walking through a town or city – look up. Look up and see what you can see. There are different stories there.

We are almost at the heart of the old Austro-Hungarian Empire. And it's Christmas. Well, technically it's Advent.

On the approach to the main square, small wooden chalet shops have been set up on Hauptplatz. There are temporary bars selling Glühwein (mulled wine) served hot and steaming, alongside established bars and restaurants. There are snacks but the place that got my attention was Nordsee fish restaurant. OK, it's part of a chain, but that does not matter for one moment. Stand at the window and look at those fantastic open sandwiches or go in a get something now. You will be tempted. Unless you don't like fish, of course. In that case, there are plenty of other places to choose. Try Lagonda, further up the road.

There is a lot of wandering, watching and photographing to do here. Alleyways and side roads to explore. Ice skating to be done in front of the town hall.

Then you arrive at the gothic Parish Church of St. Jakob (Pfarrkirche St. Jakob). This is a visit in itself. The square, a medieval cross roads, was laid out in the 12th century. The church would have had its beginnings around the same time. Walking around outside this Advent there is recorded choir music playing. Inside a high alter with rich Rococo carvings and a pulpit dating back to 1555.

St. Jakob's remains a place of worship. Holy Mass is said on Sunday 9:00 am, 10:00 am and 6:30 pm, Saturday at 9:00 am and 6.30 pm and Monday to Friday at 9:00 am and 6.30 pm. There is a Rosary daily at 6:00 pm

The Pfarrkirche (parish church) St. Jakob also offers Mass every second and fourth Sunday at 11;00 am.

For detailed and most up to date information, contact the Pfarrkirche St. Jakob directly.

Pfarrkirche Villach-St. Jakob, Kirchenplatz 8, 9500 Villach. Phone: +43 (0) 4242/24066, Fax: +43 (0) 4242/24066-5

Around the square the market stalls and wooden huts surround the church. The smell of incense drifts out of one as

I pass. Some of the crafts on sale are religious in nature, most are not.

Then in the dark the town is illuminated by beautiful seasonal lights that are strung above the street.

The rest of the year

Of course, you don't need to wait until December to visit Villach.

Advent and Christmas celebrations start over the last few days of November and run until Christmas. In 2017 a parade was held on 2 December. There is an Easter market, too, and several other events. But don't feel as if you need to find an event to attend. Villach is a good day trip from Bled.

If you wanted to stay longer than a day, particularly in the winter, there is plenty to do and see in this part of Carinthia. This is a winter sports region that provides skiing on Gerlitzen Alpe and cross country Dobratsch nature park and KärntenTherme water

park in Warmbad Villach with an adventure pool, sports pool, sauna and gym. The family-oriented water park in the most modern in Austria. It's only about 7 minutes from Villach Hbf station at Bahnhofplatz to Villach Warmbad Bahnhof.

If you are new to skiing, Gerlitzen Alp has 25 ski runs and has earned a quality seal for beginners.

For more information and confirming events and dates you will need to check with Villach Tourist Office (Tourismusinformation Villach-Stadt) at Bahnhofstrasse 3 · 9500 Villach Phone: +43 4242 2052900.

How to get there from Bled and Lesce-Bled

Train

Up to 10 times a day – but some of those times are very early in the morning or very late at night. There are a couple of morning trains to Villach and two or three returning in the afternoon. If you want to spend time exploring the town and other facilities nearby, the tourist office will help with accommodation for an overnight in Villach.

The Austrian Railways website is at *www.oebb.at/en/* (where you can download a personalised timetable). The Slovenian Railways website is *www.slo-zeleznice.si/en/* Follow link to International Time Tables

Car

The RAC website says:

"While driving in Austria you are required by law to carry the following items. Hefty on-the-spot fines can be issued for failing to carry specific items:

- Headlamp beam deflectors (depending on your car, you will either need deflector stickers or have to adjust the beam manually)
- Reflective jackets (to be used in the case of a breakdown or accident outside built-up areas, on expressways and on motorways)
- Warning triangle (all vehicles with more than two wheels registered in Austria or abroad must be equipped with a warning triangle which conforms with EC Regulation 27)
- First aid kit
- Motorcyclists (safety helmets are compulsory for drivers and passengers of mopeds and motorcycles)
- Dashboard cameras are prohibited

There Is more information about driving in Austria on the RAC website *www.rac.co.uk/drive/travel/country/austria*

Flixbus

At time of writing just once a day, check *www.flixbus.com* for up to date information.

More information about the Advent Market including events around the opening, dates and times at *www.villacheradvent.at/events/*. It's in German language, but Google Translate does a reasonably good job translating.

PART 8 -
A FEW WORDS OF SLOVENIAN

For such a small country with a population of slightly over 2 million people, the diversity of the Slovenian language is remarkable. There are somewhere between 45 and 50 different dialects (depending what reference you consult). According to the government website "dialectologists have established the presence of 46 clearly defined dialects, divided into six regional groups: Carinthian, Upper Carniolan, Lower Carniolan, Littoral, Rovte, Styrian and Pannonian."

It is said to be the most diverse Slavic Language and the first to be written down. It is one of the oldest languages in Europe.

The official website goes on to say, "It is a minority language with a recognised status as a second official language in the southern part of the Austrian province of Carinthia, in the eastern part of the Italian region of Friuli-Venezia Giulia and in the western part of the Hungarian county of Vas."

In the 1550s, Primož Trubar the Slovenian Lutheran reformer wrote the first books in Slovenian thereby consolidating the language. The diversity of the language is captured in a Slovenian proverb "Vsaka vas ima svoj glas ", meaning "every village has its own voice."

The good news is – most of the people you are going to meet in Bled and Ljubljana speak English.

If you want to dabble in the language, most people, especially in shops, restaurants and bars, respond very warmly to anyone having a go. If you get it wrong, their English will be good enough to get you through any order or purchase.

English is used as a "bridge" language in many parts of Slovenia and throughout Bled. People from non-English speaking countries – Korea, Japan, China, Russia, even France and Spain – use English as a common language.

Italian and German are spoken, too, especially further north in Kranjska Gora but it is always useful to have a few words of Slovenian. A smile and "please/prosim", "thank you/hvala", "good day/dober dan", "good-bye/adijo" will get you a long way.

Greetings

When you go into a shop, a restaurant or a bar, you will be greeted with "Dober dan." everywhere. Literally it means "Good day", the response is "Dober dan." or just "Dan".

First thing in the morning you might walk into a hotel restaurant and be greeted with "Dobro jutro" ("Good morning") or late in the evening - after dusk - "Dober večer" (pronounced "ver-chair") "Good evening". "Good night" is "Lahko noč" (pronounced "la-ko notch")

The "Hi" or "Hello" greeting is the less formal "živio". It is used among friends and especially by younger people.

So, "dober" is "good". In a restaurant, you are also going to hear "dober tek" which is "bon appetite" ... as we say in ... English.?.?

Please and thanks

"Prosim" is "please" and "hvala" is "thanks". Often in Bled you will hear people say "hvala lepa" which is the equivalent of "thank you very much". Although in other parts of Slovenia you might hear "Najlepša hvala" (pronounced "nai lepsha hwala"). And do remember to employ the "h" in "hvala" otherwise it might sound like the French "voilà"

Goodbyes and departures

The simple "adijo" ("aa - dee - o") is "'bye" but also used around Bled is the more formal "nasvidenje" – "goodbye". You will also hear "ciao". There are other "goodbye" words and phrases, but those will be enough to get you through a short visit.

Now you have enough to go into one of the Mercator shops in Bled, take something from the shelves, go to the checkout and say:

"Dober dan" ... Reply dober dan

"Prosim" ... And set down your purchases

As mentioned earlier, if you are buying loose fruit or vegetables, remember to weigh them before going to the checkout. Then hand over the money. The checkouts have a digital display of the total so you don't need to learn the numbers system ("devetnajst eurov in devetindevetdeset centov" is €19.99 ... I think.)

"Rabim vrečko" if you need a bag. "To je vse" (toy-yo-say) "That is all" or "that is everything".

Exchange "Hvala" and "Hvala lepa". Then "Adjio" all round. You'll be just like a citizen of Bled. Well perhaps not. But it will raise a smile or two.

When you are buying something in a Mercator, the person on the checkout might ask you a question with the words "Pica" and "kartica" ("Imaš pika kartico?"), you are being asked if you have a Pica card, the Mercator loyalty card. Yes "da" and no "ne".

You will pay with Euro and cents or "kreditna kartica" "credit card".

More useful words

Airport	Letališče
Airplane	Letalo
Bus	Avtobus

Car	Avto
Car Hire	Najem avtomobile
Time-Table	Vozni red
Boat	Čoln
Boat hire	Najem čolnov
Train	Vlak
Train station	Železniška postaja
Entrance	Vhod
Exit	Izhod
Left	Levo
Right	Desno
I am [name]	Jaz sem [ime]
This is [name]	To je [ime]
Let's go for coffee	Gremo na kavo
Where are the shops?	Kje so trgovine?
Tomatoes	Paradižnik
Oranges	Pomaranče
Apples	Jabolka
Lettuce	Solata
Ice cream	Sladoled
Chocolate	Čokolada

Hot chocolate	Vroča čokolada
Mulled wine	Kuhano vino
Money	Denar
How much is that?	Koliko stane?
I have the bill please?	Lahko dobim račun, prosim?

There are many useful YouTube videos to get you started.

The playlist is here: http://bit.ly/SloLessons

There is also a wonderful series on YouTube first broadcast of Radio Si Kako postaneš Slovenianc / How to become a Slovenian by Michael Manske an American journalist (bornin Germany) and executive producer of the English section of Radio Si, or Radio Slovenia International. He has lived in Slovenia since 2001

http://bit.ly/BecomeASlovenian

And don't forget Bled.tv http://bit.ly/BledTVYT

Appendix –
Other Information

To Bled from Jože Pučnik International Airport Ljubljana (Brnik)

Why, oh why is it so difficult for the independent traveller to get to Bled from the airport? And expensive, too? Yes, Bled may well be one of the principle tourist attractions in Slovenia, but getting to and from the airport is not attractive.

Here are some alternatives.

- **Call a friend.** If you are lucky enough to have friends in Bled, ask them for a lift. It will only be an hour out of their day.
- **Bus.** Awkward and time consuming but not expensive. You will need to take a bus to Kranj bus station. Buses leave on the hour (there are some service in between) and take about 20 minutes, then you will need to wait about 25 minutes for the Bled bus. Alternatively (and longer) take a bus to Ljubljana then a bus to Bled.
- **Taxi.** Likely to cost about €45. I use SMS [*www.taxi-sms.si*] phone or text +386 (0)70 999 699
- **Car Hire.** If I am with friends or family and can't cadge a lift with someone, I think that the most convenient way to get to Bled is to hire a EuropCar from the airport (always pre-book online) and return to the office in Bled. Same for the return journey. At just over £30 (paid in advance) you will have the car for 24 hours and in that time, you can do some touring around the region. Go to Vintgar, Lake Bohinj, have an evening in Ljubljana.
- Other car hire companies probably provide the same pick up at airport return to Bled office service. It's worth

169

spending a bit of time researching. But I expect they all work out a similar price.

- **Private Hire.** I asked **Marcela at Bled Tours** "What are your rates for connections from the Airport to Bled?" for details to be included in this book She told me "Personal car 1-3 passengers 55 EUR per car one way, minivan 4-8 passengers, 80 EUR per minivan, one way." Contact details for Bled Tours: Jelovška cesta 25, 4260 Bled
Mob: ++ 386 (0) 31 205 611 Tel: ++ 386 (0)4 574 35 20 www.bledtours.si and www.bled-taxi.com

- Zup Prevozi Transfers operate a shuttle service from the hotels in Bled to the airport and services from the airport to the hotels. I used it myself in May 2018. It was a good service.

Aleš Zupančič of Zup Prevozi Transfers tells me they can offer four transfer options (Economy, Economy flex, Business and VIP shuttle). Contact Aleš Zupančič, Britof 220 A, Kranj, SI-4000 Slovenia. info@zup-prevozi.eu +386 (0) 31 30 41 41

  o "Economy Shuttle: €13 per person (share ride door to door service). Departure from Airport at 11:15 or 16:45 Departure from Bled to Ljubljana Airport at 8:30 or 9:30 or 14:00 N.B. I am advised that these times are subject to change from April 2018.

  o "Economy-Flex Shuttle (flexible shuttle): When you book your Economy-FLEX, you can OPT IN to share your transfer with another couple or solo traveller. There is no fixed timetable like our Economy shuttle. The timings of our shared transfers are flexible and are timed specifically around the flight arrival or flight departure times of our clients. Journey time is approximately 30 minutes. The driver will meet you at the airport arrivals with welcome sign.

  o "Business Shuttle: (private transfer). Departure after your flight. Flexibility, comfort and reliability at your convenience. Shuttle service between airport to any location in Bled. The driver will meet you at the airport arrivals with welcome sign.

- o "VIP-luxury Shuttle: Departure after your flight. Flexibility, comfort and reliability at your convenience. Shuttle service between airport to any location in Bled. The driver will meet you at the airport arrivals with welcome sign."

- Bus to Ljubljana: Leaves on the hour and takes about an hour to get to the bus and train station in Ljubljana. Should you be so moved, you could take the bus to Kranj then train to Ljubljana – takes longer and I can't think of one good reason to do that.

Airports
Jože Pučnik International Airport Ljubljana (Brnik)

Web: *www.lju-airport.si*

Phone Passenger information: +386 4 20 61 981

E-mail: info@lju-airport.si

Maribor Airport

Web: *www.maribor-airport.si*

Phone: +386 (0)2 629 11 75

Email: info@maribor-airport.si

Bus Train and other Transport
The main bus station in Bled is convenient to the centre of town and to the main hotel and hostel area. Bled is a minor hub and is limited in direct routes. Ljubljana - naturally - is

the main hub, but Kranj, Lesce and Radovljica have important links.

Online Bus Time Table

There is what could best be described as a "quirky" timetable [*www.ap-ljubljana.si/en]* For example

- It does not list Jože Pučnik International Airport Ljubljana as a destination or departure. You need to know that the name to use is "Letališče Brnik"
- If you search for information from "Letališče Brnik" to "Bled", there is no result; "No matching connections for your request". That – presumably – is because the journey to Bled requires changing buses in Kranj. This shortcoming is a disappointment because the website was completely redesigned only a few years ago. Unfortunately, it is not tourist or visitor friendly. Best to use Google Maps (very useful, usually accurate), or find a person to ask in one of the bus stations.

Bus Operators

- Alpetour *www.alpetour.si* Phone +386 (0)4/20-13-210, promet@alpetour.si
- Arriva: *www.arriva.si* Phone 0907411 (in Slovenia)

Slovenian Railways (Slovenske železnice)

The timetable and price list for all trains in Slovenia can be found at [*www.slo-zeleznice.si/en/passenger-transport/timetable*]. Most journeys are worth taking just for the remarkable views and some amazing railway engineering.

There are two train stations: Bled Jezero above the lake on the northern shore. While convenient to the camping site, it is about a 30-minute walk to the main centre. Lesce-Bled is about 4 km from Bled centre. There is a bus. Taxis between the two towns are expensive; up to 15 EUR for a 10-minute ride.

If you are flash, there is a private airport in Lesce.

Google Trips and Google Maps

The best thing to happen to travel information in this area is the arrival of Google Trips and the ease with which you can plot your journey on a Google Map. The bus and train networks can be (very) confusing for the first-time visitor. To get from A to C you might need to connect through B. Sometimes it is difficult to know where B is. But with Google maps you can more easily find your way.

Bicycle Hire in Bled

There are lots of places to hire bikes and costs vary as do the types of bikes available. If you just want to scoot around town you should be able to pick up something inexpensive. For a more specialist model, try one of the adventure shops around the bus station.

Prices vary, even between outlets just a few paces apart. Spend a little time checking out your specific requirements. You could save yourself the price of several coffees and cakes later when you celebrate how active you have been.

Emergencies

Police emergency number 113

Ambulance emergency number 112

Bled Health Centre Mladinska cesta. 1 Tel. +386 4 575 40 00

Dental Clinic Prešernova cesta 15 +386 4 575 08 01 Opening Hours 9:00 am – 4:00 pm

Pharmacies (Lekarna)

There are two pharmacies in Bled. The main one is Lekarna Zlatorog Bled at Prešernova cesta 36. It opens most mornings at 7:30 am and closes most evenings at 8:00 pm Phone: +386 4 578 07 70

English and other languages are spoken. Carparking available.

The Marta Poljanšek Zupan lekarna in at the shopping centre facing the main road opposite the Park Hotel, Ljubljanska cesta 4. Phone: +386 4 576 60 85

Car trouble? Just a car problem or flat tire, call 1987 - AMZS (Auto-moto group, with technical centres all over Slovenia.). If you have a car crash, the police will give you the relevant information. If you have hired a car, you should have been provided with the emergency numbers by the hire company.

ATM – Cashpoint - Bankomat

- Bankomat Gorenjska Banka: cesta Svobode 15, 4260 Bled (Near promenade and Spa Park)
- SKB Bank: Ljubljanska cesta 4, 4260 Bled. (Shopping Centre)
- NLB: Ljubljanska cesta 11, 4260 Bled. (Near Union bus stop)
- Bankomat GBKR: Ljubljanska cesta 30, 4260 Bled. (Petrol station on the left going into town)
- bankomat Gorenjska banka, TC Mercator centre, Kajuhova cesta 1, 4260 Bled

Mobile Phones
You can buy a cheap disposable mobile phone in the Tuš supermarket in Lesce and from a vending machine beside the exit door at Jože Pučnik International Airport.

Wifi
Most of the cafés and restaurants have free wifi and there is free public wifi around the town centre.

About Davy Sims

Davy Sims first visited Bled in September 1996. He was working as a travel journalist with BBC reporting on Slovenia as a holiday destination. He returned several times and subsequently spent three extended periods in the town, living in Mlino, 200 metres from the lake in 2014, 2015 and 2016.

He has won broadcasting and new media awards in London, New York, Dublin and Belfast. He worked in BBC radio for most of his career, mainly in Radio Ulster but also in London as senior producer then chief producer in BBC Radio 1 and BBC Radio 4.

Davy now spends time between Northern Ireland and Slovenia. He occasionally lectures on Radio Production for Journalists in Dublin and on Journalism and Emerging Media in Ljubljana.

Davy can be found on Twitter @davysims, or through his blog davysims.com

He is also the English language voice of Bled Castle's audio-visual presentation.

Thanks

There are so many people to thank for their suggestions, ideas, inspiration and practical help. Mojca Polajnar has always been there to answer questions and help with suggestions. Tomaž Piber has been a great friend and enthusiastic supporter. But there are many more such as Lea Ferjan, Eva Štravs, Tatjana Radovic. Also, Marija, Luka, Lili, Leo, Alen, Miha and Alenka and thanks, too, to Iain and Abbi Hay. And, of course, the Mayor of Bled, Janez Fajfar. There are more. Thanks to my wife, Dawn for supporting me in these daft ideas.

Finally, thanks to everyone one who sent feedback about the book to help me amend and improve the content.

End Piece

I have tried to ensure all the details in this book are correct as of 22 May 2018. Any significant changes will be included in subsequent versions of the book. While not a fully functioning website, *www.firsthandguides.com* will point to any changes.

For continuing coverage on major events in Bled follow @LakeBledNews on Twitter

Always check with relevant websites and service providers including tourist information services before making any arrangements.

Podcasts and updates.

Check the website FirstHandGuides.com for updates, additional information and podcasts.

Twitter

For daily updates and for the Lake Bled community follow @LakeBledNews on Twitter

Other websites:

davysims.com

https://www.amazon.co.uk/Davy-Sims/e/B01LWV138Q

10227191R00096

Printed in Great Britain
by Amazon